Welcome

Welcome to this guide to modelling Great Western Railway locomotives. Despite its title, we'll be looking at all the locomotives that hauled main line express and passenger trains. Those are just the 4-6-0s, locomotives with great, curving name plates with the names of monarchs, castles, counties and stately homes of differing sizes.

The GWR is one of the most famous British railway companies and, since the late 1970s, its locomotives and wagons have dominated the ranges of the 'OO' gauge ready-to-run manufacturers. It's only when it comes to coaches do we find some significant gaps.

'N' gauge is catching up, although in the smaller scale, there are some big gaps. The same is true in 'O' gauge, although this is balanced by the superb museum-quality models available in the 'senior scale', often for a four-figure price tag and, thus, they fall outside the scope of this publication.

Flick through this guide and you'll find prototype histories, key stats and facts and, naturally being a publication for modellers, all those key detail differences that manufacturers aim to – but don't always manage, due to myriad technical reasons – include.

Of course, it must be said here that this is a general guide and there will be one-offs and odd-balls that we haven't got the space to include. If you're serious about getting into the nitty gritty of a particular class, then it's definitely recommended tracking down a good book on the subject – and being the GWR, there are plenty out there (see p114).

We also include a livery guide, a guide to the trains that these engines hauled – and how to model them – plus some projects that you might want to undertake.

So, without further ado, turn over to start immersing yourself in GWR locomotive history… and, if you enjoy it, hopefully volumes covering goods, mixed traffic and branch line engines will follow!

ABOVE: **March 4 2023 was a momentous day at Didcot Railway Centre when four restored GWR 'Castles' were gathered together for the first time at the former GWR steam shed. Resident 4079** *Pendennis Castle* **and 5051** *Drysllwyn Castle* **were joined by Vintage Trains'** 5043 *Earl of Mount Edgcumbe* **and 7029** *Clun Castle***. We'd like to thank Clive Hetherington, Great Western Society CEO and all at Didcot Railway Centre who assisted with this publication.** Jack Boskett

Contents

W.J. Reynolds/Rail Archive Stephenson/Rail Online

Contents

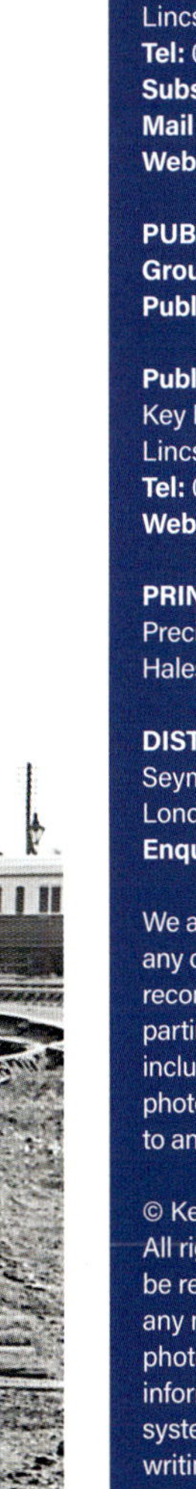

ISBN: 978 1 83632 179 8
Editor: Richard Foster
Senior editor, specials: Roger Mortimer
Email: roger.mortimer@keypublishing.com
Design: SJmagic DESIGN SERVICES, India
Cover design: Steve Donovan
Advertising Sales Manager: Sam Clark
Email: sam.clark@keypublishing.com
Tel: 01780 755131
Advertising Production: Becky Antoniades
Email: Rebecca.antoniades@keypublishing.com

SUBSCRIPTION/MAIL ORDER
Key Publishing Ltd, PO Box 300, Stamford,
Lincs, PE9 1NA
Tel: 01780 480404
Subscriptions email: subs@keypublishing.com
Mail Order email: orders@keypublishing.com
Website: www.keypublishing.com/shop

PUBLISHING
Group CEO: Adrian Cox
Publisher: Steve O'Hara

Published by
Key Publishing Ltd, PO Box 100, Stamford,
Lincs, PE9 1XQ
Tel: 01780 755131
Website: www.keypublishing.com

PRINTING
Precision Colour Printing Ltd, Haldane,
Halesfield 1, Telford, Shropshire. TF7 4QQ

DISTRIBUTION
Seymour Distribution Ltd, 2 Poultry Avenue,
London, EC1A 9PU
Enquiries Line: 02074 294000.

What makes GWR locomotives so special?

ABOVE: **George Jackson Churchward** (1857-1933). STEAM Picture Library

ABOVE: **Frederick William Hawksworth** (1884-1976). STEAM Picture Library

That's a difficult question to answer. The Great Western Railway has a magic about it that attracts devotees willing to defend it with a fanaticism possibly only matched by those who follow the locomotive designs of the London & North Eastern Railway's legendary designer Sir Nigel Gresley.

The GWR represents a long-gone world, a quieter, simpler time before the technology-led 21st century; a time of sleepy villages amidst green and pleasant hills, of cricket on the green, cream teas and the pint of something medicinal at the pub.

The GWR was unique among British railway companies. It was formally launched as the Bristol & London Railway at Bristol Guildhall on July 30 1833, changing its name to 'Great Western Railway' later that year. The bill, to build a railway from London to Bristol, received royal assent on August 31 1835.

The origins of the Railways Act 1921 were laid when the UK government took control of the railways during the First World War. It didn't want to return to having the railways owned by myriad companies as had existing before 1914; likewise, it didn't want full nationalisation.

The result was to group the railway companies into four large conglomerates. Three, the LNER, London Midland & Scottish and Southern Railways, would be new companies and with the GWR were known as the 'Big Four'. However, of the 'Big Four', the GWR had unique status. It was given the status of an 'amalgamated company' and would continue to operate as it had before the war but, from January 1 1922, would start to absorb the smaller companies that had been allocated to what had been the called 'the Western Group'.

This gave the GWR a great advantage. There was none of the infighting that permeated the LMS and LNER, as old rivals now had to work together.

The GWR continued to innovate – it sowed the seeds of the Diesel Multiple Unit and it implemented widespread Automatic Train Control safety systems to name but two – and its publicity machine worked with a ferocity that would make a modern advertising agency green with envy.

There were two men responsible for its individuality. The first was the legendary engineer Isambard Kingdom Brunel. Brunel was still relatively inexperienced when he was appointed engineer to the GWR. He called it the "finest work in England" but his vision went beyond building a railway between London and Bristol.

He wanted to link London with New York and he would design Atlantic-crossing ships as well as a railway. And it wouldn't just be a railway; it would be the world's first high speed railway. It would be as straight and level as possible and a track gauge of 7ft ¼in would give stability to trains running at higher speeds.

Sadly, the GWR would be forced to relinquish the last of its broad gauge in 1892. But, by then, its lines and trains would stretch from London as far west as Penzance. Its network would reach the south coast and Wales while thanks to cooperation with other railways, its trains would go as far north as Crewe and Nottingham.

The other man to shape the GWR was George Jackson Churchward. Outwardly, he was the typical Victorian country gent. He enjoyed fishing and hunting. A bachelor, he respected his household staff and his joviality ensured he commanded the respect from those around him.

But under this façade was a remarkable engineer. He joined the South Devon Railway as an engineering apprentice in 1871, moving to Swindon when the GWR took over the SDR in 1876. He rose through the ranks to become Chief Assistant to Locomotive Superintendent William Dean in 1897. Dean retired through ill health in 1902 and Churchward succeeded him.

Churchward had his own views on the ingredients for the best possible locomotives. But, unlike Brunel who had supreme confidence in his own ability, Churchward liked to test his ideas. He also had no qualms about incorporating the ideas of others even if – and here he set himself apart – they were American in origin. Or French!

What made Churchward so important to GWR locomotive practice was that having put together the best locomotive possible,

ABOVE: **Charles Benjamin Collett** (1871-1952). STEAM Picture Library

he used the parts and ideas to design a *range* of locomotives. Manufacturing techniques at Swindon Works were improved and the works itself expanded to accelerate production. And, finally, new sheds and repair centres were built to keep these new engines in top order. Indeed, from 1902 until the end of the 1920s, the GWR really led the way in British locomotive design and production.

Churchward retired as Chief Mechanical Engineer at the end of 1921, Charles Benjamin Collett taking over the job on January 1 1922. The two men couldn't have been more different, Collett more aloof and insular than Churchward. That's why Churchward's tragic death on December 19 1933 – he was hit by a train – was keenly felt around Swindon.

Collett, as we'll see, initially pushed the boundaries of GWR locomotive development. He'd joined the GWR in 1893 and rose through the ranks as Churchward was embarking on his ambitious journey. But, as the 1930s progressed, Collett began to focus increasingly on the study of the spiritual and the paranormal. There was nothing essentially wrong with his locomotive output but other railways began to overtake in terms of technological innovation.

Great things were expected of his successor, Frederick Hawksworth. But he became Chief Mechanical Engineer at the height of the Second World War and any thoughts he might have had to modernise things had to play second fiddle to simply getting the GWR back on its feet.

The GWR had continued to plough its own furrow through the 1930s and 1940s and would do so when it became part of the British Railways at Nationalisation on January 1 1948. The newly formed Western Region fought tooth and nail to continue to manufacture tried and tested GWR designs rather than new BR Standards, but it was in vain.

The Western then became one of the regions that pushed hardest to get rid of steam. It managed to almost achieve this on January 3 1966 when 'Modified Hall' No. 6998 *Burton Agnes Hall* hauled what was claimed to be the Western Region's last steam service – an Oxford-Banbury service.

It's probably fair to say that Western Region individuality – and thus Great Western Railway individuality – finally came to an end in February 1977 when the last of the 'Western' diesel hydraulics were withdrawn.

RIGHT: Low down is the best way to appreciate the awesome power and mammoth lines of the GWR 'King'. The driver of 6015 *King Richard III* oils round while the fireman watches the photographer. This photograph was taken in the yard at Swindon Works after a General overhaul (May 13 1937-July 3 1937). Rail Archive Stephenson/Rail Online

Designer	Charles Collett
Lifespan	1927-1962
GWR power class	E (BR '8P')
GWR route restriction	Double Red

We start with the epitome of Great Western Railway express power. The mighty 'Kings' took the principles laid down by Churchward to the absolute limit.

Some might argue that the 'Kings' were unnecessary. They were hampered by their huge bulk and the earlier 'Castles' – see page 28 – could pretty much do every job a 'King' could.

But that misses the point of the 'Kings'. They were a status symbol and the choice of name reflected that. When new in 1927, they truly were the kings of the rails.

The seeds of the 'King' had actually been sown at the British Empire Exhibition at Wembley in 1924. This vast undertaking was designed to reinvigorate a Britain still living in the shadows of the First World War. The GWR had exhibited pioneer 'Castle' 4073 *Caerphilly Castle* with the declaration that it was Britain's most powerful steam locomotive. Impossible, said the London & North Eastern Railway, for our new 'A1' 4-6-2 is clearly bigger and thus more powerful.

Both companies decided to find out. A 'Castle' was sent to the LNER and a Gresley 'A1' 4-6-2 went to the GWR. And the 'Castle' came out on top. While LNER designer Nigel Gresley went back to the drawing board to improve his engine, the GWR milked the publicity for all it was worth.

So, imagine its consternation when, in 1926, the Southern Railway popped up with a locomotive more powerful than the 'Castle'. And then there were rumours that the last of

The 'King' 4-6-0

the 'Big Four' railways, the London Midland & Scottish Railway, were also working on a new express engine.

The biggest limitation to designing a new locomotive was its weight and the forces transferred to the track and bridges. The 'Castle' had offered an increase in power over its predecessors but the weight increase was negligible. However, in order to top the 40,000lb tractive effort that GWR General Manager Felix Pole demanded, the new engine must be heavier. Happily, the chief Civil Engineer J.C. Lloyd acceded to an axle weight increase of 22½ tons on the London-Plymouth route.

Collett's design team got to work on the new project. The boiler became a larger version of the Standard No. 1 and the cylinders were increased in bore and stroke. In order for the inside cylinders to fit, a new bogie was designed, with the bearings on the leading axle on the outside of the frames, while the trailing axle's bearings remained on the inside.

With the tractive effort tantalisingly close at 39,100lb, Collett opted for slightly smaller driving wheels. Legend has it that he was inspired by witnessing a GWR mixed traffic 2-6-0 out-accelerating an express 4-6-0. The new 6ft 6in diameter driving wheels resulted in a tractive effort of 40,290lb.

The first of the new engines was unveiled in June 1927. This was important for the GWR had been invited to exhibit an engine at the centenary celebrations of the Baltimore & Ohio Railroad in the USA that autumn. The newly christened 6000 *King George V* was quickly packed off to North America where it wowed the crowds, despite being much smaller than the engines the Americans were used to.

Back home, the 'Kings' settled down to hauling the GWR's premier expresses to the West Country.

'KING' – KEY DIMENSIONS

Dimensions	Prototype	1:76 scale	1:148 scale	1:43 scale
Length (over buffers)	68ft 2in	273.5mm	140.4mm	483.4mm
Height (over chimney)	13ft 4¾in	53.7mm	27.5mm	94.9mm
Width (over cylinders)	8ft 11½in	36mm	18.5mm	63mm
Wheel diameter (driving)	6ft 6in	26.4mm	13.5mm	46.2mm
Wheel diameter (bogie)	3ft 0in	12mm	6.1mm	21mm
Wheel diameter (tender)	4ft 1½in	16.4mm	8.4mm	28.7mm
Cylinders (4)	16¼in by 28in	-	-	-

ABOVE: W.J. Reynolds/Rail Archive Stephenson/Rail Online

NUMBERS AND BUILDS

Engine Nos.	Lot No.	Building dates	Works/Builder
6000-6019	243	June 1927-June 1928	Swindon
6020-29	267	May 1930-August 1930	Swindon
6007*	309	Mar-36	Swindon

* No. 6007 was written off in an accident at Shrivenham, just to the east of Swindon on January 15 1936. The engine was officially renewed – heavily rebuilt – at Swindon, hence the new Lot number.

WHERE WERE THEY SHEDDED?

Shed name	GWR Code	BR code
Bristol Bath Road	BRD	82A
Cardiff Canton*	CDF	86C (1950-1960
		88C (1960-1963)
Newton Abbot	NA	83A
Old Oak Common	PDN	81A
Plymouth Laira	LA	83D
Wolverhampton (Stafford Road)	SRD	84A

'King' liveries

1927-1928
Nos. 6000-6004 only

1928-1934

1934-1940

1940-1947

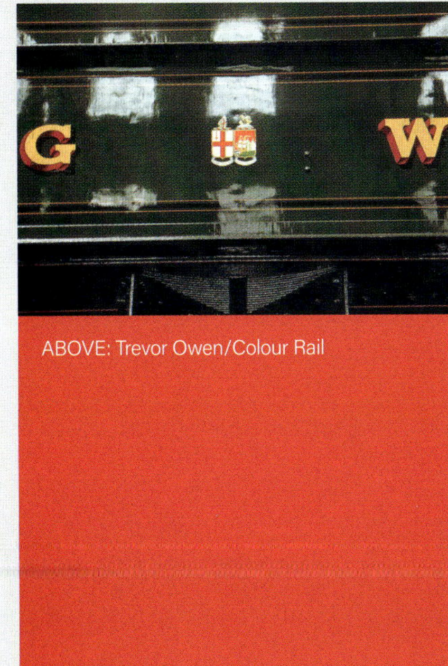

ABOVE: Trevor Owen/Colour Rail

1948-50

1950-1956

1956-1962

'King' tenders

Collett 4,000gal from new

ABOVE: Colour Rail

CAN I SEE ONE?

The 'Kings' were withdrawn between June and December 1962. Three survive: 6000 *King George V* (STEAM – Museum of GWR at Swindon); 6023 *King Edward II* (Didcot Railway Centre); 6024 *King Edward I* (Locomotive Services Ltd, Crewe).

Model timeline

1980	Hornby's new 'OO' gauge tender-drive 'King' joins that from Lima, new the previous before.
1993	Last time Lima offers its 'OO' gauge 'King'.
2000	New 'N' gauge 'King' from Graham Farish. In reality, it's the existing 'Castle' model with a newly tooled bogie.
2003	Hornby reveals a new, Chinese-made version of the tender-drive 'King', now with the motor in the locomotive. Last time Graham Farish 'King' appears in the catalogue.
2015	All new, 21st century standard model from Hornby with 21-pin DCC socket and NEM couplers. Sound available.
2020	KR Models proposes 'N' gauge 'King', after previous DJ Models scheme; both schemes have come to naught.
2025	models available

Hornby R30364 6009 *King Charles II*, BR green
Hornby R30363 No. 6029 *King Stephen*, GWR green

RRP: £249.99. Availability: Hornby stockists or *www.hornby.com*

'King' detail differences

1 Feed pipes

ABOVE: **6000-6019 had straight top feed pipes when new.**

ABOVE: **6020-6029 built with curved top feed pipes. 6000-6019 later changed; all modified by end of 1934.**

2 Bogie springs

LEFT: **Original bogie spring arrangement (6000-6005).**

BELOW: **Later spring arrangement (6006 onwards).** R Broughton/Colour Rail

3 Inside valve chest

ABOVE: **Original curved top and valve spindle covers (6000-6019).** W.J. Reynolds/Rail Archive Stephenson/Rail Online

ABOVE: **Later valve spindle cover (6020-6029)**

4 Smokebox door

A: Top lamp iron moved from top of smokebox to smokebox door from 1932 onwards

B: Door step added c1930. Started to be removed from 1932 onwards.

5 Tender filler

6000-6019 had twin tender filler lids; 6020-6029 had single filler (as illustrated). Tenders later modified to single filler.

ABOVE: P. Fabricius/Colour Rail

7 Oil covers

Additional cover over oil pipe on driver's side added in 1930s. Removed when four-row superheaters fitted in 1949.

6 Speedometer

ABOVE: **Jaeger speedometers fitted to 6006/07/10/17/23/25/26 from 1933.** Rail Archive Stephenson/Rail Online

ABOVE: **Whole class fitted with standard GWR speedometer by 1937.**

8 Early 1950s condition 'King'

A: Four-row superheater with enlarged oil pipe cover from 1948.
B: Chequered plate top to inside cylinders, from c1948.
C: Mechanical lubricators (original position) from 1949 (only 23 'Kings' had lubricators here).

RIGHT: Trevor Owen/Colour Rail

9 Final condition 'King'

A: Cab roof ventilators added from 1954
B: Whistle shields introduced from 6006 onwards
C: Double chimney and blastpipe fitted from 1955
D: Raised top to centre cylinder cover after strengthening ribs added, early 1950s onwards
E: Final position of mechanical lubricator
F: Revised shape steampipes from 1953 onwards.

RIGHT: K.L. Cook/Rail Archive Stephenson/Rail Online

Designer	George Jackson Churchward
Lifespan	1902-1953
GWR power class	C (BR '4P')
GWR route restriction	Red

ABOVE: Surely a case for the adage 'if it looks right, it is right'? 2937 *Clevedon Court* rests in the centre road at Hereford on July 22 1952, perfectly showing off the handsome lines of a 'Saint' in final condition. The engine has less than a year left for it was withdrawn on June 22 1953. Even at this time, these engines were still capable of some superb performances but had been made redundant by new 'Castles', 'Counties' and 'Modified Halls'.
R.O. Tuck/Rail Archive Stephenson/ Rail Online

Archaeopteryx, the winged dinosaur discovered in the early 1860s, is generally considered by palaeontologists to be the link between dinosaurs and modern birds. If there is a locomotive equivalent, it's this, the Great Western Railway's 'Saint'.

The fitting of 2901 *Lady Superior* with a superheater in 1906 was a watershed moment in British locomotive design for it set the standard for all future two-cylinder 4-6-0s. It had a large, efficient boiler, long travel valves – and the addition of a superheater was the icing on the cake. Here was the modern locomotive. Everything before it belonged to locomotive pre-history, steam-powered dinosaurs.

There was a direct line from the 'Saints': they led to the GWR 'Hall' and from that came the LMS 'Black Five'. That, in turned, inspired the LNER 'B1' and both designs came together in the BR Standard '5MT' of 1951. The 'Castles' can trace their lineage to the 'Saints' and they would impact LMS and LNER locomotive development while Harold Holcroft, Churchward's protégé, would take 'Saint'-like thinking with him to the South Eastern & Chatham Railway (and thence the Southern) in 1914.

O.S. Nock falls just short of naming them "the greatest-ever steam locomotive in British practice," saying "on the grounds of... capacity for maximum output in relation to nominal tractive powers, the Great Western

The Saint 4-6-0

'Saint' must be very nearly second to none, if not entirely without rivals." Kenneth Leech said that they were his favourite GWR 4-6-0 while Didcot fireman Harold Gasson called them "beautiful."

For all their beauty and grace, they're a difficult class to describe, mainly because, like Archaeopteryx, the design evolved. We've listed the class here as comprising 77 examples but that includes all the prototypes and odd batches that Churchward built while he experimented. You can learn more about them on p25.

Yet even the story of the production 'Saints' is confusing, thanks to the evolution of what would become the Standard No. 1 boiler. There were short-coned boilers, different length smokeboxes

and then, in 1912, the missing piece in puzzle, in the form of top feed. Here, water was fed into the boiler on perforated 'trays' via the steam space. This not only gave an element of pre-heating but also helped filter out any impurities.

The information you'll see over the next few pages reflects the final evolution of the 'Saint' design. If you want specific information on earlier versions and prototypes then it's definitely worth checking out the myriad books written about the development of the class.

There is something about the early engines that we can't ignore. The GWR 4-6-0 design might look antiquated to us in 2025 but it caused shockwaves in the Edwardian era. British locomotives were *styled*.

Churchward's were too austere and, with the high running plates, too *American*.

Harold Holcroft solved the aesthetic issue by dropping the level of the cab sidesheets and running board and then linking it to the running board with a sweeping curve. There was a similar curve at the front end. But what this meant was that when straight frame engines needed new cylinders, hybrid 'Saints' were born with a mixture of styles!

As seminal as the design was, it was quickly superseded and the class disappeared before the preservation movement was born. Happily, the Great Western Society didn't want the 'Saint' legend to die and built a new one, so future generations can see a live one. Unlike Archaeopteryx.

'SAINT' – KEY DIMENSIONS

Dimensions	Prototype	1:76 scale	1:148 scale	1:43 scale
Length (over buffers)	63ft ¼in	252.6mm	129.7mm	441.4mm
Height (over chimney)	13ft 3¼in	53.3mm	27.3mm	93.1mm
Width (over cylinders)	8ft 11in	36mm	18.5mm	63mm
Wheel diameter (driving)	6ft 8in	27.2mm	14mm	47.6mm
Wheel diameter (bogie)	3ft 2in	12.8mm	6.5mm	22.4mm
Wheel diameter (tender)	4ft 1½in	16.4mm	8.4mm	28.7mm
Cylinders (2)	18½in by 30in	-	-	-

ABOVE: L.R. Tomsett/Rail Archive Stephenson/Rail Online

NUMBERS AND BUILDS

Engine Nos.	Lot No.	Building dates	Built
100 (2900)	132	1902	Swindon
98 (2998)	138	1903	Swindon
171 (2971)	145	1903	Swindon
172-180 (2972-2980)	154	1905	Swindon
181-190 (2981-2990)	158	1905	Swindon
2901-2910	164	1906	Swindon
2911-2930	170	1907	Swindon
2931-2940	185	1911	Swindon
2941-2950	189	1912	Swindon
2951-2955	192	1913	Swindon
Total built: 77 (including prototypes)			

CAN I SEE ONE?

Withdrawals started in 1931 and the last, 2920 *Saint David*, was withdrawn on October 5, 1953. There is a story that 2937 *Clevedon Court* was bought by the owner of the namesake house but was scrapped when it wouldn't fit up his driveway. The Great Western Society bought 'Hall' 4942 *Maindy Hall* from Barry in 1974 with the express purpose of turning it into a 'Saint.' That dream was completed in 2019 and it's why you won't find 2999 *Lady of Legend* listed in Table 3.

WHERE WERE THEY SHEDDED?

Shed name	GWR Code	BR code
Banbury	BAN	84C
Bristol Bath Road	BRD	82A
Cardiff Canton*	CDF	86C
Chester West	CHR	84K
Ebbw Junction	NA	83A
Exeter	EXE	83A
Fishguard Goodwick	FDG	81A
Gloucester Horton Road	GLO	83D
Hereford	SRD	84A
Leamington	LMTN	84D
Newton Abbot	NA	83A
Old Oak Common	PDN	81A
Plymouth Laira	LA	83D
Pontypool Road	PPRD	86G
Reading	RDG	81D
Shrewsbury	SALOP	84G
Swansea Landore	LDR	87E
Swindon	SDN	82C
Taunton	TN	83B
Tyseley	TYS	84E
Westbury	WES	82D
Weymouth Radipole	WEY	82F
Wolverhampton Stafford Road	SRD	84A
Worcester	WOS	85A

'Saint' liveries

1902-c1905

ABOVE: Colour Rail

c1905-1928

1928-1934

1934-1940

1940-1947

ABOVE: Trevor Owen/Colour Rail

1948-53

'Saint' tenders

Churchward 3,500gal short fender

ABOVE: Rail Online

Churchward 3,500gal long fender

Collett 3,500gal tender

ABOVE: H.N. James/Colour Rail

Model timeline

1986   Hornby modifies the old 1960s Tri-ang 'Hall' tooling to produce a curved-frame 'Saint'. It's heavily compromised but remains in production until the late 1990s.

2024   Hornby answers the wishes of many GWR modellers when it announces that it is to produce an all 'Saint'. The first models depict straight-frame 'Saints' but curved-frame will surely follow.

2025   Models available to pre-order:
Hornby R30404 No. 2999 *Lady of Legend*, GWR garter crest
Hornby R30405 No. 2975 *Lord Palmer*, GWR green
RRP: £234.99. Availability: Hornby stockists or *www.hornby.com*

Early condition 'Saint' – 1

A: Original straight frames
B: Saturated boiler with short smokebox
C: Coned boiler
D: No top feed (introduced from 1912
E: Original rear frame and step arrangement

ABOVE: Rail Online

Early condition 'Saint' – 2

A: Cast iron chimney (from 1919)
B: Lamp iron on top of smokebox
C: Superheated: extended smokebox and covers for oil pipes
D: Half-coned boiler
E: Tall safety bonnet, with top feed
F: Cab porthole windows (covered from c1928)
G: Lever reverser

ABOVE: Colour Rail

Final condition 'Saint' – 1

A: Rear curved frame and footsteps (from 1912)
B: Screw reverser (from 1912)
C: Short safety valve bonnet (introduced 1927)
D: Front curved frame (from 1912)

Final condition 'Saint' – 2

A: 'Grange' chimney (introduced 1939)
B: Lower top lamp iron (introduced 1932)
C: Automatic train control (introduced from 1908)
D: Outside steam pipes (introduced from 1930)
E: Four cone ejector (introduced from 1913)
F: Speedometers (introduced 1937, selected engines)
G: Whistle shields (introduced 1925)

ABOVE: Colour Rail

ABOVE: Trevor Owen/Colour Rail

The gas turbines

Designer	Frederick Hawksworth
Lifespan	1950-1973
GWR power class	N/a
GWR route restriction	N/a

It's easy to forget that for all its traditions, the GWR was a forward-thinking company. As the 1930s progressed, it continued to invest in diesel railcars, building up an enviable fleet by the time BR was formed in 1948. Plans to electrify the London-Bristol main line were curtailed by the Second World War.

After the war, the LMS and Southern Railway both started to develop main line diesel locomotives while the LNER implemented its electrification scheme on the Woodhead Route across the Pennines. But the GWR pursued a different tack, thanks to a chance encounter in Switzerland.

The Swiss unveiled the first gas turbine locomotive in 1939, the 'Am 4/6 1101'. It worked by having an air compressor force air into a combustion chamber where fuel was injected. The air-fuel mixture was ignited and the gases turned a turbine, which then powered an electrical generator. This generator fed electricity to the traction motors, akin to a traditional diesel electric.

Maybe it was an 'Am 4/6 1101' that Frederick Hawksworth saw when on an visit to Switzerland, but he quickly realised the potential for gas turbine power on the Great Western. Returning to the UK, the GWR placed an order with Swiss Locomotive & Machine Works and Brown-Boveri for a 2,500hp locomotive in 1946.

The GWR was likely to have come under intense political scrutiny for placing an order with an overseas manufacturer while British industry was trying to rebuild itself after the Second World War. Another order was placed for a gas turbine locomotive shortly after the SLM/Brown-Boveri one, this time with Metropolitan Vickers. The Swiss locomotive's 2,500hp was deemed equivalent to the power output of a 'King'; the Metro-Vick locomotive was to have 3,000hp.

Building both locomotives was a time-consuming process and construction was still on-going in Switzerland and Manchester when the Great Western Railway effectively ceased to exist following the creation of British Railways on January 1 1948.

It wouldn't be until the start of a new decade before both locomotives entered service. The Swiss locomotive, 18000, started work in May 1950 while the Metro-Vick, 18100, followed suit on March 4 1952.

Both locomotives spent long periods at Swindon, often with minor faults and this tainted their working lives. They were powerful locomotives and swiftly able to recover if checked by signals. 18000 was probably the better performer and was clocking up mileages between shopping on a par with a 'Castle' 4-6-0.

But those niggling faults combined with a move towards diesel hydraulic traction would end the Western's gas turbine experiment. 18000 was withdrawn in 1960

and returned to Switzerland where it was converted into a test bed by the Office for Research & Experiments (ORE) of the International Union of Railways. It returned to Britain in the 1990s and was cosmetically restored to original black and silver livery at Tinsley depot, near Sheffield. Owned by record producer Pete Waterman, it's been displayed at Crewe and Barrow Hill, where it was repainted into BR green. Now at Didcot Railway Centre, it's gradually being conserved and restored to its original livery.

18100 was returned to Metropolitan Vicker's factory at Dukinfield, Manchester, in 1955. It returned to BR service in October 1958 having been rebuilt as 25kV electric locomotive, No. E1000. Re-numbered E2001 in October 1959, it would eventually find use as a crew trainer on the electrified sections of the West Coast Main Line in Cheshire and Scotland. Allocated Class 80 on BR's TOPS system, it never received its 80001 number for it was withdrawn in 1968 and scrapped in late 1972/early 1973.

18000 - KEY DIMENSIONS				
Dimensions	Prototype	1:76 scale	1:148 scale	1:43 scale
Length (over buffers)	63ft 0in	252.6mm	129.7mm	441.4mm
Height	13ft 4in	53.7mm	27.5mm	93.8mm
Weight	8ft 7¾in	35.2mm	18.1mm	61.6mm
Wheel diameter (driving)	4ft ½in	16mm	8.3mm	28mm
Wheel diameter (unpowered)	3ft 2in	12.8mm	6.5mm	22.4mm
Bogie wheelbase	12ft 10in	48.2mm	24.9mm	84.7mm

NUMBERS AND BUILDS			
Engine Nos.	Lot No.	Building dates	Works/Builder
18000	372	1946-1949	SLM/Brown-Boveri
18100	388	1946-1951	Metropolitan-Vickers
Total: 2			

18100 - KEY DIMENSIONS				
Dimensions	Prototype	1:76 scale	1:148 scale	1:43 scale
Length (over buffers)	66ft 8in	267.9mm	137.5mm	468mm
Height	13ft 6in	54.5mm	28mm	95.2mm
Width	9ft 0in	36mm	18.5mm	63mm
Wheel diameter	3ft 8in	15.2mm	7.83mm	26.6mm
Bogie wheelbase	15ft 0in	60.1mm	30.8mm	105.1mm

18000 liveries

1950-1956

ABOVE: Trevor Owen/Colour Rail

1956-57

ABOVE: Trevor Owen/Colour Rail

1957-1960

LEFT: Colour Rail

18100 liveries

1951-1955

ABOVE: Colin Marsden Collection/Colour Rail

1955-73

ABOVE: Colour Rail

Available models

Heljan joined forces with Rails of Sheffield to develop ready-to-run 'OO' gauge models of both 18000 and 18100. Both companies went the whole hog and even offered 18100 in its later electric form as E1000/E2001.

The 18000 project was announced in 2019 and the model went on sale in 2021. It was an immediate sell-out and you can only find them second-hand.

18100 was announced in 2021 and it arrived in stock in the summer of 2024. A slower seller than 18000, versions are still available from Rails of Sheffield (0114 2551 436 or *www.railsofsheffield.com*).

The prototype 4-6-0s

The 'Saints' were what in today's parlance would be called a 'game changer'. But Churchward didn't get to the final design overnight. Here's the story of the prototypes…

The first signs that Swindon Works was up to something came in 1901 when Dean 'Single' 3021 *Wigmore Castle* was fitted with fake outside cylinders. It made its way around the GWR network, checking that a locomotive with outside cylinders – hitherto unknown on the GWR – would fit.

All was revealed the following year when 100 appeared from Swindon Works. It was unlike anything the GWR – or any other British railway company – had built before.

Where to start? The 'Badminton' 4-4-0s had become the first GWR locomotives to be fitted with a Belpaire firebox. Belgian engineer Alfred Belpaire had developed this in the 1860s and its virtue was to maximise the water circulating over the hottest part of the fire.

Mounting the regulator valve – the 'tap' through which steam from the boiler passes to the cylinders – in a dome atop the boiler limited the boiler's size. A dome on a big boiler would strike bridges and tunnels.

Fitting the regulator in the smokebox enabled the boiler diameter to be enlarged. Move the safety valves moved to where the

dome would be and such a boiler was fitted to 'Badminton' 3310 *Waterford*.

The 'Atbara' 4-4-0s adopted this boiler together with a drumhead smokebox. This is where the smokebox was held in a saddle rather than extending up from the frames.

Prototype 100 had a longer version of the 'Atbara' boiler, the new No. 1. It also had outside cylinders. These were cast with the smokebox saddle and the steam passages into two halves, being bolted back to back to form a complete unit. Inside Stephenson's valve gear was retained but were linked to the outside cylinders by rocking levers.

What grabbed the attention – aside from its American lines – was the 30in stroke. This, Churchward said, was the only way he knew to give a simple engine the thermal efficiency of a compound. For while this locomotive appeared while William Dean was still in charge at Swindon, the design was all Churchward.

As revolutionary as 100 was, it was not the finished article. Contemporary train timers recorded superb performances on level sections of line but somewhat indifferent hill

climbing. But Churchward was not done yet and a second 4-6-0, No. 98, was built the following year, quickly followed by a third… and then more.

Each prototype featured further refinements in design while the story is complicated by the fact that Churchward had yet to decide whether a 4-6-0 was any better than a 4-4-2.

These prototypes would pave the way for the 'Saints' of 1906 (p14). And, eventually, the prototypes, even 100, were grouped under the 'Saint' banner. This complicates the 'Saint' story. So let's take a closer look just at the prototypes over the page.

100	
Built	February 1902
'Saint' No.	2900 *William Dean*
Withdrawn	June 1932

The first Churchward 4-6-0. See p25 for full details.

RIGHT: Robert Brookman/Rail Archive Stephenson/ Rail Online

ABOVE: Rail Archive Stephenson/Rail Online

98	
Built	May 1903
'Saint' No.	2998 *Ernest Cunard*
Withdrawn	June 1933

This boasted two further innovations. It had a taper to the rear of the boiler, increasing its diameter in order to ease the transition to the firebox and to allow more water to circulate. The internals of the boiler were different, featuring fewer yet larger boiler tubes. It also had larger piston valves and, to accommodate them, Churchward used North American-style bar frames at the front end. These were incorporated into the cylinder-smokebox saddle castings to create a whole front frame assembly.

TABLE 1: THE CHURCHWARD PROTOTYPES					
Original No.	**Built**	**Final No.**	**Final name**	**Rebuilt as 4-6-0**	**Withdrawn**
171	Dec-03	2971	*Albion*	1907	Jan-46
172	Mar-05	2972	*The Abbot*	1912	Mar-35
173	Mar-05	2973	*Robins Bolitho*	N/a	Mar-33
174	Apr-05	2974	*Lord Barrymore*	N/a	Aug-33
175	Apr-05	2975	*Lord Palmer*	N/a/	Nov-44
176	Apr-05	2976	*Winterstoke*	N/a	Jan-34
177	Apr-05	2977	*Robertson*	N/a	Feb-35
178	May-05	2978	*Charles J. Hambro*	N/a	Nov-46
179	Apr-05	2979	*Quentin Durward*	1912	Mar-51
180	Jun-05	2980	*Coeur de Lion*	1913	Jul-48
181	Jun-05	2981	*Ivanhoe*	1912	May-51
182	Jul-05	2982	*Lalla Rookh*	1912	Jun-34
183	Aug-05	2983	*Redgauntlet*	1912	May-46
184	Aug-05	2984	*Guy Mannering*	1912	May-33
185	Jul-05	2985	*Peveril of the Peak*	1912	Aug-31
186	Jul-05	2986	*Robin Hood*	1912	Nov-32
187	Aug-05	2987	*Bride of Lammermoor*	1912	Oct-49
188	Aug-05	2988	*Rob Roy*	1912	May-48
189	Sep-05	2989	*Talisman*	1912	Sep-48
190	Nov-05	2990	*Waverley*	1912	Jan-39
98	Apr-03	2998	*Ernest Cunard*	N/a	Jun-33

171	
Built	December 1903
'Saint' No.	2971 *Albion*
Withdrawn	January 1946

This engine was a virtual copy of 98 but with one difference: the boiler pressure was raised from 200lb/sq in to 225lb/sq in. This raised the tractive effort from 20,000lb to 23,000lb and was done in response to the purchase of the French engine, 102. This became the standard GWR boiler pressure for express engines but whether it would have been if Churchward had not chosen to try out his designs against 102, we'll never know.

To make a more direct comparison, 171 was rebuilt as a 4-4-2 in October 1904. It became a 4-6-0 again in 1907.

ABOVE: Rail Archive Stephenson/Rail Online

172 *Quicksilver*	
Built	March 1904
'Saint' No.	2972 *The Abbot*
Withdrawn	March 1935

This was the first new 4-4-2 and was virtually identical to the rebuilt No. 171.

173-178	
Built	March-April 1905
'Saint' Nos.	See Table 1
Withdrawn	See Table 1

These engines were built as 4-6-0s, virtually identical to the original No. 171.

RIGHT: Rail Archive Stephenson/Rail Online

179-190	
Built	April 1905-July, 1907
'Saint' Nos.	See Table 1
Withdrawn	See Table 1

All built as 4-4-2, with half-cone boilers. The majority of these engines, together with some of the 4-6-0s, would receive full cone boilers – with the taper extending closer to the smokebox – circa 1909. Half-cone boilers with superheaters were fitted a few years later and then, just before the start of the First World War, full-cone superheated boilers were fitted.

RIGHT: Robert Brookman/Rail Archive Stephenson/Rail Online

The 'Castle' 4-6-0

Designer	Charles Collett
Lifespan	1923-1965
GWR power class	D (BR '7P')
GWR route restriction	Red

What exactly can one say about the GWR 'Castle' 4-6-0? If you follow the route of progression in terms of increasing the 'size of a GWR 4-6-0, it goes 'Saint', 'Star' and then 'King'. The 'Castle' was more of a side-step of that route along that route... but it arguably produced the better locomotive.

GWR management managed to overlook how much it cost to build Churchward's engines when they realised what a publicity coup it was to have Britain's most powerful locomotive. But new 4-6-0s and 4-6-2s from the Lancashire & Yorkshire, Great Northern and North Eastern Railways had taken that title away from Swindon.

Collett's first task as Chief Mechanical Engineer was to build a bigger version of the 'Star' in order to win back that honour. Churchward had spent his final years at Swindon wrestling with that problem but his proposals for fitting the 'Star' chassis with the No. 7 boiler from a '47XX' 2-8-0 simply wouldn't fit the loading gauge.

The solution was a halfway house between the 'Star's' No. 1 boiler and a No. 7. The No. 1 barrel's diameter was increased by 3in.

ABOVE: The Great Western Railway is synonymous with moving large numbers of holiday makers to the coastal resorts of Devon and Cornwall. Many a holiday started with a ride behind one of the superlative 'Castles', although this group are seemingly oblivious to 5011 *Tintagel Castle* as it passes with the 10.45am Manchester-Plymouth on July 7 1959. Peter Gray/Rail Archive Stephenson/Rail Online

The firebox was also increased in length but the amount of water that was allowed to circulate was reduced in order to increase the size of the grate. The backplate also tapered towards the top, unlike the No. 1.

Collett and his team looked at a couple of other areas too. The valve gear was tweaked

and outside steampipes not only improved the flow of steam to the cylinders but made maintenance much easier.

Aesthetically, Collett got it right, too. A new cab, larger than anything Churchward had offered, beautifully complemented the bigger boiler. The result was a very pretty machine with a tractive effort of 31,625lb; the Great Northern Railway's new 4-6-2s, designed by H. N. Gresley, could only boast 29,835lb.

The GWR's publicity machine went into overdrive. Pioneer 4073 *Caerphilly Castle* was displayed at Paddington station soon after it was outshopped in August 1923 and a complementary new book was published that sold over 40,000 copies in a matter of months. This success was built upon when

Caerphilly Castle was displayed at the 1924 British Empire Exhibition as 'The Most Powerful Express Locomotive in Britain.'

The GWR and LNER decided to find out if that was true. Trials on both railways took place between April 27 and May 2 1925. 4074 *Caldicot Castle* out-performed 'A1' 4474 *Victor Wild* on the GWR but the true shock was that No. 4079 knocked No. 2545 *Diamond Jubilee* into a cocked hat on LNER turf, even while burning hard northern coals. The 'Castles' performed better and used less coal and it convinced Gresley that longer travel valves were the future. He would use this knowledge when creating the 'A3s' and streamlined 'A4s.'

The 'Castle's' reputation was cemented the following year when the LMS secured the

loan of 5000 *Launceston Castle.* It performed beautifully between London and Carlisle.

What impressed the LMS most was what E.S. Cox described as its "quiet mastery." *Launceston Castle* wasn't being thrashed like a 'Claughton' to accelerate 415 tons from 20mph at Shap summit to 66mph at Tebay and nor was it gobbling coal.

The events of May 9 1964 were the perfect send off for this magnificent design. The high speed train, running 60 years after *City of Truro* reached 100mph featured some superb 'Castle' performances but, sadly, the magic 'ton' wasn't reached. Still, the efforts of that day helped ensure that there were still 'Castles' around to celebrate the class's centenary in 2023.

Dimensions	Prototype	1:76 scale	1:148 scale	1:43 scale
Length (over buffers)	65ft 1¾in	260.8mm	134.2mm	456.8mm
Height (over chimney)	13ft 5½in	54mm	27.8mm	94.5mm
Width (over cylinders)	8ft 11½in	36mm	18.5mm	63mm
Wheel diameter (driving)	6ft 8½in	27.2mm	14mm	47.6mm
Wheel diameter (bogie)	3ft 2in	12.8mm	6.5mm	22.4mm
Wheel diameter (tender)	4ft 1½in	16.4mm	8.4mm	28.7mm
Cylinders (4)	16in by 26in	-		

ABOVE: J.P. Wilson/Rail Archive Stephenson/Rail Online

NUMBERS AND BUILDS			
Engine Nos.	Lot No.	Building dates	Works/ Builder
4073-4082	224	1923-24	Swindon
4083-4092	232	1925	Swindon
4093-5012	234	1926-1927	Swindon
5013-5022	280	1932	Swindon
5023-5032	295	1934	Swindon
5033-5042	296	1935	Swindon
5043-5067	303	1936-37	Swindon
5068-5082	310	1938-39	Swindon
5083-5092*	317	1937-1940	Swindon
5093-5099**	324	1939	Swindon
7000-7007	357	1946	Swindon
7008-7027	367	1948-49	Swindon
7028-7037	375	1950	Swindon
Total: 166			

* Rebuilt from 'Stars' Nos. 4063-4072
** Nos. 5098/99 not built until 1946

'Castle' liveries

1923-1928

1928-1934

1934-1940

1940-1947

ABOVE: Trevor Owen/Colour Rail

1948-1956

1956-1965

WHERE WERE THEY SHEDDED?		
Shed name	**GWR code**	**BR code**
Banbury	BAN	84C
Bristol Bath Road	BRD	82A
Bristol St Philips Marsh	SPM	82B
Cardiff Canton	CDF	86C
Cardiff East Dock	CED	88B
Carmarthen	CARM	87G
Chester West	CHR	84K
Didcot	DID	81E
Ebbw Junction	NA	83A
Exeter	EXE	83A
Fishguard Goodwick	FDG	81A
Gloucester Horton Road	GLO	83D
Hereford	SRD	84A
Llanelli	LLY	87F
Neath Court Sart	NEA	87A
Newton Abbot	NA	83A
Old Oak Common	PDN	81A
Oxford	OXF	81F
Penzance	PZ	83G

(CONT'D)		
Shed name	**GWR code**	**BR code**
Plymouth Laira	LA	83D
Reading	RDG	81D
Severn Tunnel Junction	STJ	86E
Shrewsbury	SALOP	84G
		89A (1960-1963)
		6D (1963-1967)
Southall	SHL	81C
Stourbridge Junction	STB	84F
Swindon	SDN	82C
Swansea Landore	LDR	87E
Taunton	TB	83B
Truro	TR	83F
Tyseley	TYS	84E
Westbury	WES	82D
Weymouth Radipole	WEY	82F
Wolverhampton Oxley	OXY	84B
Wolverhampton Stafford Road	SRD	84A
Worcester	WOS	85A

'CASTLE' REBUILDS

Not all the 'Castles' were built new. Aside from 'Stars' Nos. 4063-72 rebuilt between 1937 and 1940, the following engines were rebuilt as 'Castles':

No.	'Castle' Name	Built as	Built New	Date Rebuilt
111	*Viscount Portal*	4-6-2 *The Great Bear*	Feb-08	Sep-24
4000	*North Star*	Four-cylinder 4-4-2	Apr-06	Nov-29
4009(a)	*Shooting Star*	'Star' 4-6-0	May-07	Apr-25
4016(b)	*The Somerset Light Infantry (Prince Albert's)*	'Star' 4-6-0	Apr-08	Oct-25
4032	*Queen Alexandra*	'Star' 4-6-0	Oct-10	Apr-26
4037(c)	*The South Wales Borderers*	'Star' 4-6-0	Dec-10	Jun-26

(a) Became No. 100A1 *Lloyds* in January, 1936
(b) Named *Knight of the Golden Fleece* until January 1938
(c) Named *Queen Philippa* until April 1937

CAN I SEE ONE?

The 'Castles' were withdrawn between 1950 and 1965. Eight survive, although it's likely that 7027 *Thornbury Castle* will be broken for spare parts. The others are located as follows: 4073 *Caerphilly Castle* (STEAM–Museum of GWR at Swindon), 4079 *Pendennis Castle* (Didcot Railway Centre), 5029 *Nunney Castle* (Locomotive Services Ltd, Crewe), 5043 *Earl of Mount Edgcumbe* (Tyseley Locomotive Works), 5051 *Earl Bathurst* (DRC), 5080 *Defiant* (TLW) and 7029 *Clun Castle* (TLW).

'Castle' tenders

Collett 3,500gal

Churchward 3,500gal

Collett 4,000gal

Hawksworth 4,000gal

Model timeline

1982   Graham Farish introduces new 'N' gauge 'Castle', joining a 'OO' gauge model from GMR Airfix that was new in 1979.
1983   The ex-Airfix 'Castle' re-appears under the Dapol brand, the new Winsford-based business tooling an all-new Hawksworth tender to complement the Airfix model.
1996   Dapol sells its 'OO' gauge range to Hornby, including the 'Castle'. It returns to the market in 1997.
2003   Bachmann re-introduces the old Graham Farish 'Castle' under its 'Graham Farish by Bachmann' brand.
2009   The first of Hornby's all-new 'OO' gauge 'Castle' lands in model shops; more arrive in 2010.
2016   Bachmann's all-new Graham Farish 'N' gauge 'Castle' hits the shelves for the first time.
2025   Hornby teases the possibility of 'Castle' being part of its 'TT:120' range.

Hornby 'Castles': 2025
- R30402   5081 *Lockheed Hudson*, GWR 1940s livery
RRP: £229.99. Availability: Hornby stockists or *www.hornby.com*

Graham Farish 'Castles': 2025
- 372-031A   5015 *Kingswear Castle*, BR lined green
- 372-034   5055 *Earl of Eldon*, G crest W lined green
- 372-035   4082 *Windsor Castle*, GWR shirt button
RRP: From £179.95. Availability: Bachmann stockists

Detail differences

LEFT: W.J. Reynolds/Rail Archive Stephenson/Rail Online

4073

A: Bogie brakes (4073-4082 removed c1925)
B: Roof gutter (4073 only)
C: Tall single chimney (4073-5043)
D: Porthole windows (4073-5005), plated over from c1928

4000

A: Running plate is slightly higher than on other 'Castles', a legacy of being fitted with scissors valve gear. The running plate is level with the top of the inside cylinders; it's lower on a production 'Castle'.

ABOVE: Colling Turner/Rail Archive Stephenson/Rail Online

1 Inside cylinder covers

Narrow fluted cylinder covers (4073-4092 and 1920s rebuilds)

Wider fluted cylinder covers (4093-5012)

Box cylinder cover (5013-7037 including 1930s rebuilds)

BR strengthening cylinder cover (selected engines, 1950s onwards)

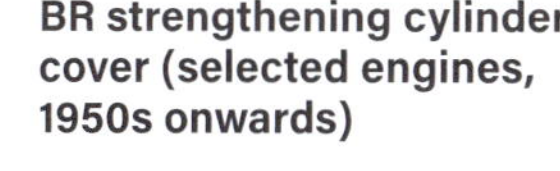

2 Spindle covers

Early valve spindle covers

Later valve spindle cover (5013 onwards)

3 Frames

Joggled frames (4073-4092)

Dished frames (4093 onwards)

4 Superheaters

Two row superheater

Three row superheater (5098 onwards)

Four-row superheater (selected locos from 1947 onwards)

ABOVE: Rail Photoprints

ABOVE: Rail Photoprints

ABOVE: Norman Preedy Collection/Rail Photoprints

5 Mechanical lubricator (7000 onwards). Later fitted to double-chimney engines

6 Chimneys
Original chimney

Short single chimney (5044-7037)

Double-chimney (selected engines from 1957 onwards)

7 Spectacle glasses

Standard size

8 Steampipes

Original steampipes

Curved steampipes (1956 onwards)

9 Sandboxes

Original sandboxes

Introduced from 5058 onwards; later fitted to selected engines

Wide spectacle plate windows (5013-5062)

10 Fire iron tunnel

No fire iron tunnel

Fire iron tunnel, 5013 onwards. Fitted to earlier engines.

11 Top lamp iron

Lamp iron on top of smokebox door

Lamp iron moved to smokebox door (5023 onwards)

12 Cabside handrails

Straight handrails (4073-5097)

Angled handrail (5098 onwards)

13 Balance weight

Small balance weight

Large balance weight

14 Bogie footstep

1923-c1960

Bogie footsteps removed c1960

ABOVE: **What a vision of beauty! This fabulous portrait shows off the elegant lines of a Dean '3031', in this case 3047 *Lorna Doone*. These engines are often known as 'Achilles' after the name given to pioneer 3031.**
Rail Archive Stephenson/Rail Online

Designer	William Dean
Lifespan	1894-1915
GWR power class	N/a
GWR route restriction	N/a

"Though the later and larger classes to come… may have been of more imposing and powerful appearance, nothing has approached the 4-2-2 class of Dean in beauty of line and appearance."

So wrote Harold Holcroft, who would ultimately be responsible for the look of the 20th century Great Western steam locomotive when he added simple curves to link the front footplate and running boards of Churchward's designs.

He was not wrong. William Dean's '3031' series of 'singles' were beautiful machines. Yet beneath that beauty was a strong and efficient locomotive.

The 'single' – a locomotive with a single driving axle with large diameter driving wheels – dated back to the early days of the GWR when Daniel Gooch was in charge of locomotive matters. This was after Isambard Kingdom Brunel found there was something that he couldn't do – design locomotives.

The GWR had kept hold of two of its most famous 'singles', *North Star* and *Lord of the Isles*, both built to its idiosyncratic 7ft ¼in gauge, until 1906. Broad gauge had been abandoned in 1892 and the GWR forced to adopt 4ft 8½in 'standard gauge'.

The 'single' was the *de facto* standard express engine for many British railway companies during the mid-19th century. The next logical step was to add a second set of driving wheels, from the which larger designs - 2-4-0s and 4-4-0s - evolved.

Yet, in the 1890s, the GWR was still building 'singles'. William Dean, then Locomotive

The '3031' 4-2-2

Superintendent, introduced the '3001' class of 2-2-2s in 1891. Holcroft explains that 'singles' offered smoother running than a coupled locomotive, that they consumed less coal and were easier to maintain. Heavier section rail allowed more weight to be placed over the driving axle to maximise adhesion, while steam-powered sanding proved more efficient at reducing slippage than gravity sanding.

When a '3001' snapped a leading axle, it was decided to rebuild them as 4-2-2s, using a modified version of Dean's carriage bogie, as this also allowed access to the cylinders. The opportunity was taken to reduce the bore from 20in to 19in, while the cab was reduced in width, the springs for the rear axle being mounted on the running plate where the cab side sheets were once affixed.

Authorisation was given to build a further 50 to this modified '3001' design. These became the '3031' class, the zenith of GWR 'single' technology.

The 50 '3031s' were built between 1894 and 1899, the last of them being almost obsolete even as they were being built. George Jackson Churchward, who'd moved to Swindon from the South Devon Railway in 1876, became Dean's Chief Assistant in 1897. Dean's health was failing while Churchward had ideas of his own that he was itching to try out. Indeed, as the final 4-2-2s were being built, a new 4-6-0, 2601, appeared. It was ugly and not hugely efficient but it did enable Churchward to try out one or two things, ruling some out and modifying others. Indeed, in 1900, 'single' 3027 *Worcester* received what would become Churchward's No. 2 boiler.

Rebuilding the class took place between 1905 and 1906 but the influx of new 'Saints' and 'Stars' rendered them redundant and the last was withdrawn in 1915.

It's easy to dismiss the 'singles' as a Victorian dinosaur. Yet 3065 *Duke of Connaught* ran from Bristol to Paddington in just 99 minutes 46 seconds on May 9 1904. It was then the fastest time set between the two cities and 'Castle' 7018 *Drysllwyn Castle* would only shave six minutes off that with the fastest 'Bristolian' timing in 1958.

Dimensions	Prototype	1:76 scale	1:148 scale	1:43 scale
Length (over buffers)	N/a	N/a	N/a	N/a
Height	N/a	N/a	N/a	N/a
Width	N/a	N/a	N/a	N/a
Wheel diameter (driving)	7ft 8½in	31.2mm	16mm	54.6mm
Wheel diameter (bogie)	4ft 1in	16.4mm	8.4mm	28.7mm
Wheel diameter (trailing)	4ft 7in	18.8mm	9.6mm	32.9mm
Cylinders (2)	19in x 24in	-	-	-

BELOW: Rail Archive Stephenson/Rail Online

NUMBERS AND BUILDS			
Engine Nos.	Lot No.	Building dates	Works/Builder
3031-3040	94	1894	Swindon
3041-3060	95	1894	Swindon
3061-3080	110	1897-1899	Swindon
Total: 50			

CAN I SEE ONE?

Princess Helena became the last '3031' to be withdrawn in December 1915. None survived but when Madam Tussauds needed a replica locomotive for its 'Royalty and Railways' exhibition at Windsor & Eton Central station, it commissioned Steamtown, Carnforth, to build a replica of 3041 *The Queen*. The non-working reproduction moved to Windsor in 1982. It's still at the station, even though the exhibition closed in 1997 and the tender was subsequently scrapped.

'3031' liveries

1894-c1905

C1905-1915

ABOVE: Colour Rail

Available models

This is a story that's probably unique in British-outline ready-to-run. Tri-ang introduced its new 'OO' gauge version of 3046 *Lord of the Isles* in 1961. It made sporadic catalogue appearances, even into the 1980s, by which time Tri-ang had become Hornby Railways (an epic story in its own right that is, sadly, beyond the scope of this publication!).

Hornby made a surprise decision in the mid-2000s. It re-tooled *Lord of the Isles'* chassis, adding a DCC decoder. Retaining the original body moulds, the model returned to the shelves, this time as other Dean '3031s'. It then moved to the Railroad range circa 2020 and often returns to the catalogue.

Detail differences

Note that bogie, driving and trailing wheels were increased by ½in from 1898

Original condition

ABOVE: Rail Archive Stephenson/Rail Online

Rebuilt version

A: Taper boiler with Belpaire firebox and drumhead smokebox fitted circa 1908
B: Churchward cab with porthole spectacle windows

RIGHT: Rail Archive Stephenson/Rail Online

The 'County' 4-6-0

Designer	F.W. Hawksworth
Lifespan	1945-1964
GWR power class	D (BR '6P')
GWR route restriction	Red

The famed author and railway authority O.S. Nock tells the story that, during the war years, there was a feeling around the Great Western Railway that it ought to consider building some sort of powerful locomotive for hauling heavy trains once the war was over. He tells how Chief Draughtsman Frank Mattingly told the Swindon design team to start working on a 4-6-2, the GWR's first since *The Great Bear*. It would be a mixture of traditional Swindon practice with some technological advances, inspired by the work of Andre Chapelon.

There was a rumour that the class was to be called 'Cathedrals', the original proposed name for the 'Kings', but an artistic impression in Nock's seminal *The GWR Stars, Castles & Kings* bears the name *Lord of the Isles*.

There must have been a bit of disappointment when the first all-new post-war class appeared in 1946 as a two-cylinder 4-6-0.

Frederick Hawksworth's first all-new tender locomotive was a product of its time. Britain was just emerging from the devastating Second World War, which had taken a debilitating toll on its railways. On the LMS and LNER, maximising power and efficiency with minimum frills and fuss was the order of the day. Only Southern Railway Chief Mechanical Engineer Oliver Bulleid felt confident to try out new things, with his air-smoothed 4-6-2s.

The GWR followed the LMS and LNER. The 'County's' frames were virtual copies of the 'Modified Halls'; the boiler was a 'Swindonised' version of the LMS '8F' boiler that the GWR had built during the war. But the pressure was upped to a whopping 280lb/sq in and the first engine even sported a double chimney. Reducing the driving wheel diameter to 6ft 3in maximised the power output.

There was a new tender, an all-welded job; welding came to the fore during the war, in place of costly riveting. The new tenders were also wider, which meant that the cab was wider than the GWR standard and crews didn't take to the removal of the thin toe-hold at the bottom of the cab sidesheet.

Externally, the 'Counties' had all the design cues of a Great Western 4-6-0. Only the tender and continuous splashers added a touch of post-war modernity.

Hawksworth was upset when the railway press revealed that his new locomotives would be numbered in the 99XX series. So, he hurriedly re-arranged matters so that the first engine became 1000.

The 'Counties' have always divided opinion. They were initially poor steamers, gobbled coal and then gained a reputation for rough riding.

It was only 1000 that was fitted with a double chimney from new. Fitting the

class with double chimneys and reducing the boiler pressure to 250lb/sq in ironed out some of the issues, but the reputation for coal consumption and rough riding continued. But crews discovered a lot of power and a sure-footedness. These were engines capable of holding their own against the 'Castles' and even the 'Kings'.

How good were they? We haven't seen a 'County' since 1964. But the Great Western Society is building a new one using the frames of 'Modified Hall' 7927 *Willington Hall*. And when the re-created 1014 *County of Glamorgan* takes to the rails, we'll get to see how good they were.

BELOW: **Despite still carrying its single chimney, 'County' 1012** *County of Denbigh* **puts on a volcanic display as it climbs Dainton, one of the fearsome south Devon banks between Newton Abbot and Plymouth, with a Down express on September 9 1955. It would be fitted with a double chimney in September 1957.**
R.O. Tuck/Rail Archive Stephenson/Rail Online

Dimension	Prototype	1:76 scale	1:148 scale	1:43 scale
Length (over buffers)	63ft ¼in	252.6mm	129.7mm	441.4mm
Height (over cab)	13ft 2½in	53.7mm	27.5mm	93.8mm
Width (over cylinders)	8ft 11⅛in	36mm	18.5mm	63mm
Wheel diameter (driving)	6ft 3in	25.2mm	12.9mm	44.1mm
Wheel diameter (bogie)	3ft 0in	12mm	6.1mm	21mm
Wheel diameter (tender)	4ft 1½in	16.4mm	8.4mm	28.7mm
Cylinders (2)	18½in by 30in	-	-	-

BELOW: Norman Preedy/Rail Photoprints

NUMBERS AND BUILDS

Engine Nos.	Lot No.	Building dates	Works/Builder
1000-1029	358	1945-1947	Swindon
Total: 30			

WHERE WERE THEY SHEDDED?

Shed name	GWR code	BR code
Bristol Bath Road	BRD	82A
Bristol St Philips Marsh	SPM	82B
Carmarthen	CARM	87G
Chester West	CHR	84K
Didcot	DID	81E
Exeter	EXE	83A
Hereford	SRD	84A
Newton Abbot	NA	83A
Neyland	NEY	87H
Old Oak Common	PDN	81A
Penzance	PZ	83G
		84D (from 1963)
Plymouth Laira	LA	83D
Shrewsbury	SALOP	84G
St Blazey	SBZ	83E
Swindon	SDN	82C
Truro	TR	83F
		84C (from 1963)
Westbury	WES	82D
Weymouth Radipole	WEY	82F
Wolverhampton Stafford Road	SRD	84A

'County' liveries

1945-1949

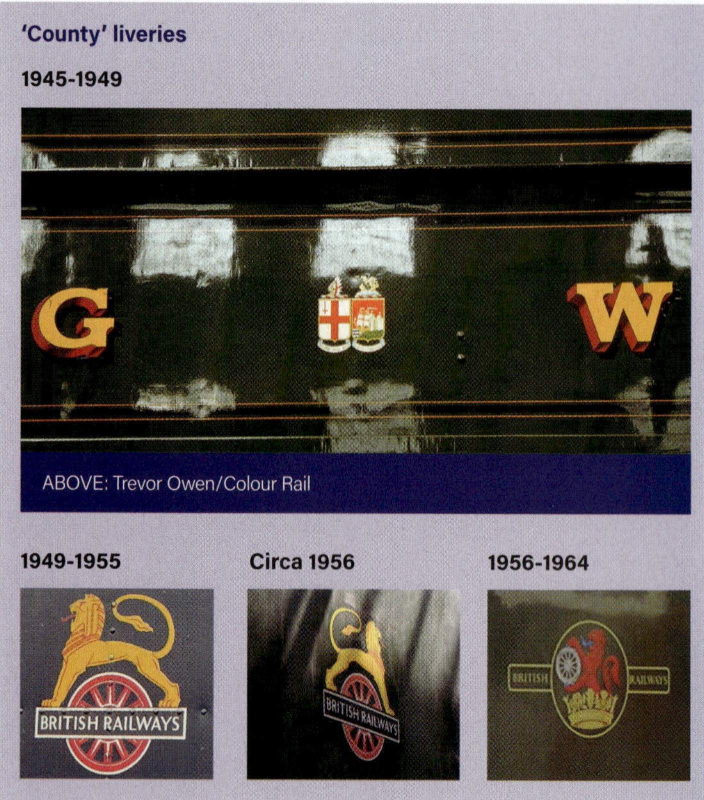

ABOVE: Trevor Owen/Colour Rail

1949-1955   **Circa 1956**   **1956-1964**

CAN I SEE ONE?

The last 'County' – 1011 *County of Chester* – was withdrawn on November 6 1964 and the whole class scrapped. A replica of 1014 *County of Glamorgan* is under construction at Didcot Railway Centre.

'County' tenders

Model timeline

1985 — Dapol uses the old Airfix 'Castle' as the basis for a new 'OO' gauge 'County' 4-6-0.

1997 — Dapol's 'County' tooling is sold to Hornby in 1996; the model returns in Hornby packaging this year.

2010 — Having been fitted with a DCC socket in 2005, the old Dapol 'County' becomes part of Hornby's budget Railroad range this year.

2025 — Rapido Trains UK announces that it is to produce an all-new 'OO' gauge 'County'.

Hornby 'Counties' available

R30376 *County of Merioneth* Train Pack

RRP: £179.99. Availability: Hornby stockists or *www.hornby.com*

Rapido 'Counties' available
- 954001   1001, GW green
- 954002   1005 *County of Devon*, GW green
- 954003   1017 *County of Hereford*, British Railways green
- 954004   1019 County of *Merioneth*, BR black early
- 954005   1013 *County of Dorset*, BR black early
- 954006   1006 *County of Cornwall*, BR green early
- 954007   1014 *County of Glamorgan*, BR green early
- 954008   1021 *County of Montgomery*, BR green late
- 954009   1000 *County of Middlesex*, BR green late
- 954010   1011 *County of Chester*, BR green late

RRP: From £249.95. Availability: Rapido Trains UK stockists or *www.rapidotrains.co.uk*

Detail differences

1 Chimneys

Double chimney – 1000 (1945-1958)

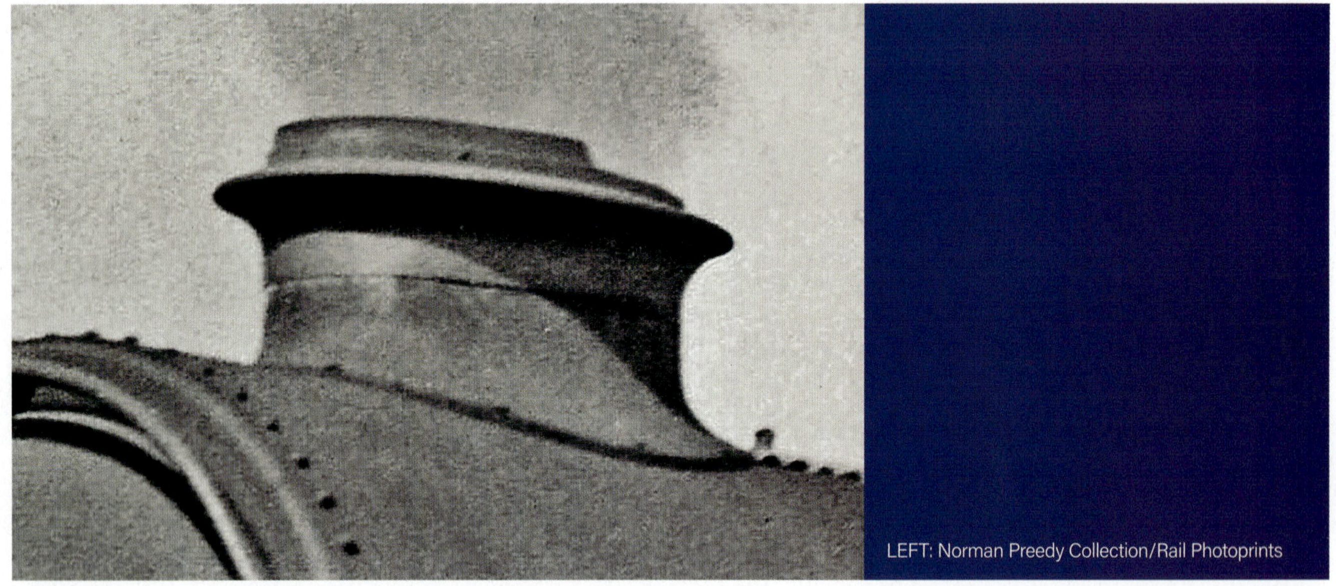

LEFT: Norman Preedy Collection/Rail Photoprints

Single chimney (1945-1959)

Double chimney (1956-1964)

ABOVE: Neville Simms/Ranwell Collection/Rail Photoprints

2 Speedometer

Fitted between 1950 and 1954

3 **Superheaters**

Original three-row superheater

Four row superheater fitted from 1957

EARLYBIRD DISCOUNT
BOOK NOW - PAY 2025 PRICES!

THE

GREAT ELECTRIC
TRAIN SHOW

October 10/11 2026
Arena MK, Milton Keynes
MK1 1ST

BOOK NOW AND SAVE WITH OUR EARLYBIRD DEAL!

Book before **December 31 2025** to get GETS tickets at 2025 prices. Use code **EARLYBIRDGETS26** at checkout.

keymodelworld.com/greatelectrictrainshow

908/25

The 'Double frame' 4-4-0s

They were the GWR's prime express design around the turn of the 20th century. But don't worry if you can't tell the difference between a 'Duke' and an 'Atbara'? You soon will...

C ritics will be quick to point out that all GWR locomotives look the same. Those in the know can respond accordingly, citing the myriad differences between, say, a 'Hall' and a 'Manor'. But there is one family of Great Western locomotive where spotting those differences is not so easy.

Welcome to the world of the 'Double frame' 4-4-0s.

Before we get into the individual classes, a locomotive with 'double frames' has just that: one set of frames inside the wheels and one set outside of the wheels. You can usually spot them by the fact that the driving wheels are hidden but the coupling rods and cranks are clearly visible, rather like a Class 08 diesel shunter.

ABOVE: **A GWR 'Double frame' 4-4-0 – but what is it? It's 'Bulldog' 3346** *Godolphin*, **photographed near Hayes circa 1900, one of the class built new with curved frames. Turn the page for a guide to identifying these similar looking machines.**
Rail Archive Stephenson/Rail Online

This was a common feature during the Victorian era. The National Collection's Midland Railway 2-4-0 156A has double frames, for example. Harold Holcroft explained that although it was more expensive to build locomotives with double frames – and it increased the weight – it permitted larger cylinders or steam chest and provided very generous bearing and big end surfaces.

The baulk road, the longitudinal timbers of Brunel's broad gauge, had survived the gauge conversion of 1892 because a section was removed from the transoms and one running line was literally pushed closer to the other to make a 4ft 8½in gauge railway. But as the 1890s progressed, the GWR began to replace the baulk road with conventional sleepered track, capable of taking heavier and more powerful machines. And thus, the GWR built its first 4-4-0s, the 'Armstrongs', in 1894. From this quartet came the 'Dukes'... and all the subsequent GWR 'Double framers'.

'Duke'	
Designer	Dean
Introduced	1895
Numbers (pre-1912)	3252-3291, 3313-3331
Numbers (post-1912)	3252-3291
Numbers (1946)	9054/64-65/72-73/76/83-84/87/89/91
Driving wheel diameter	5ft 8in
Boiler	Duke
Frame	Curved
Last withdrawn	1951
Survivors	Officially, the boiler from 3258 *The Lizard* survives on 'Dukedog' 9017 at the Bluebell Railway.

Notes

B4 boilers fitted from 1903.

Top feed, superheating and piston valves fitted 1911-1915; Churchward smokebox doors fitted from 1920s

There were narrow and wide types of cabs, the latter further widened to suit the Churchward 3,500gal tender.

ABOVE: Steve Armitage Archive/Rail Online

'Badminton'	
Designer	Dean
Introduced	1897
Numbers (pre-1912)	3292-3311
Numbers (post-1912)	4100-4119
Wheel diameter	6ft 8½in
Boiler	No. 2
Frame	Curved
Last withdrawn	1931
Survivors	N/a

Notes

These were effectively a larger wheeled version of the 'Duke'. They also had 18in by 26in cylinders and were the first GWR engines to be fitted with a Belpaire firebox.

ABOVE: Rail Archive Stephenson/Rail Online

'Bulldog'	
Designer	Dean
Introduced	1899
Numbers (pre-1912)	3332–3352-72, 3413–32 and 3443–72
Numbers (post-1912)	3300-3440
Wheel diameter	5ft 8in
Boiler	Standard No. 2
Frame	Curved; shallow
Last withdrawn	1949
Survivors	Frames from No. 3425 survive under No. 9017

Notes

Nos. 3300-3340 were originally built as 'Dukes' and have curved frames. Frame fractures led to the distinctive straight frame – as illustrated right – to be introduced from 1900.

Parallel boilers were replaced by half-cone and taper versions. Some 'Bulldogs' were fitted with No. 3 boilers from withdrawn '36XX' 2-4-2Ts.

Topfeed, superheaters and piston valves fitted 1910-1925.

Cab side-sheets flared from 1930.

ABOVE: Rail Online

'Atbara'	
Designer	Dean
Introduced	1900
Numbers (pre-1912)	3373-3412
Numbers (post-1912)	4120-4148
Wheel diameter	6ft 8½in
Boiler	No. 2
Frame	Straight, shallow
Last withdrawn	1931
Survivors	N/a

Notes

A larger wheeled version of the 'Bulldog'.

Parallel No. 2 boiler later replaced by half-coned and then full-coned boiler.

Frames strengthened between 1905 and 1907. Ten rebuilt with No. 4 boiler to become 'City' (see p50).

ABOVE: Robert Brookman/Rail Archive Stephenson/Rail Online

'Flower'	
Designer	Churchward
Introduced	1908
Numbers (pre-1912)	4101-4120
Numbers (post-1912)	4149-4168
Wheel diameter	6ft 8½in
Boiler	No. 2
Frame	Straight, deep
Last withdrawn	1931
Survivors	N/a

Notes
These engines, all named after flowers, were built with the coned No. 2 boiler as standard. They were identical to the 'Atbaras' except for that they had screw rather than steam reversers and that the outer frames were made deeper to give them more strength.

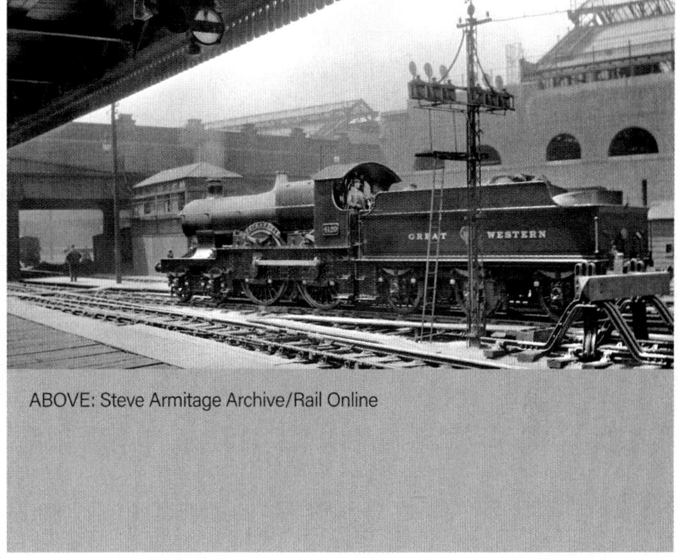

ABOVE: Steve Armitage Archive/Rail Online

'Bird'	
Designer	Churchward
Introduced	1909
Numbers (pre-1912)	3731-3745
Numbers (post-1912)	3441-3455
Wheel diameter	5ft 8in
Boiler	Standard No. 2
Frame	Straight, deep
Last withdrawn	1951
Survivors	N/a

Notes
As the 'Flowers' were taper boiler and deep-frame versions of the 'Atbara', so the 'Birds' – guess what they were named after? – were taper boiler and deep-framed versions of the 'Bulldogs'. Like the 'Flowers', they had screw reversers rather than steam reversers.

ABOVE: C.A.J. Nevitt/Rail Archive Stephenson/Rail Online

The 'City' 4-4-0

Designer	George Jackson Churchward
Lifespan	1902-1931
GWR power class	A
GWR route restriction	Blue

Did it, or didn't it? This is the question that has divided opinion since May 9 1904: did 3440 *City of Truro* become the first British locomotive to do 100mph?

There was intense rivalry between the GWR and the London & South Western Railway over who could offer the fastest service between London and Plymouth. The GWR had the contract to move mail from incoming ships from North America, while passengers went via the LSWR.

The arrival of SS *Kronprinz Wilhelm* at Plymouth on May 9 1904 sparked such a race. Mail was transferred to a train headed by GWR 'City' 3440 *City of Truro*. On the footplate, driver Moses Clements was at the regulator, in the company of inspector G.H. Flewellen. On board was noted train timer Charles Rous-Marten and it was he who timed *City of Truro* at what was later calculated to be 102.3mph.

As the only timer on board, we only have Rous-Marten's evidence. O.S. Nock analysed the feat and believed "a maximum speed of at least 100mph may be accepted on *City of Truro's* behalf".

What is certain is that the 'Cities' were capable of some fast running. On April 9 1904, classmate *City of Exeter* ran an ocean mail and topped Whiteball summit at 60mph compared with 'Truro's' 52mph. That was one of a series of fast runs that 'Exeter' made, while Nock says that's *City of Gloucester's* run on May 2 1904 would have been the fastest ever, had 'Truro' not made that high speed dash a few days later.

The reason why the 'Cities' became such speed machines was due to the boiler.

Churchward designed four new boilers. The No. 1 boiler was designed for his new 4-6-0 (see p25). The No. 2 boiler was for the 'Atbara' 4-4-0s and 'Aberdare' 2-6-0s. Then came the No. 3, which was a No. 2 with a 9in shorter barrel. This was designed for the short-lived '36XX' 2-4-2Ts.

Then, in 1902, 'Atbara' 3405 *Mauritius* was fitted with a new boiler. The barrel and firebox were the same length as the No. 2 but the barrel was 6in wider as was the firebox as it used the same throat and backplate as the No. 1. This new boiler became the No. 4 and its success was an increased heating surface and the greater capacity for steam and hot water.

Ten new No. 4-fitted 'Atbaras' were ordered in 1903. They were named after cities and that's how the class would be referred to thereafter. Given their success, a further nine 'Atbaras' were rebuilt in 1907-1908.

Given how quickly the GWR was re-stocking its fleet of express locomotives, it's surprising that the 'Cities' lasted as long as they did. But the construction of more 'Castles' led to 'Saints' being released for secondary duties. This work was the mainstay of the double-framed 4-4-0 fleet. And then, rebuilding *Saint Martin* with 6ft diameter driving wheels and the subsequent creation of the 'Halls' sounded the death knell.

The Railway Magazine was delighted that the LNER managed to provide a home for 'Truro' in its museum at York, claiming that "not yet is the romance of the railway quite dead." The LNER claimed that 'Truro' was the first locomotive to top the 'ton'… that was until its own *Flying Scotsman* reportedly did the same in 1934.

LEFT: **Arguably the GWR's most famous locomotive, 4-4-0 3440 *City of Truro*, steams through Sydney Gardens, Bath, with the RCTS' 'North Somerset Railtour' on April 28 1957.** Hugh Ballantyne/Rail Photoprints

Dimensions	Prototype	1:76 scale	1:148 scale	1:43 scale
Length (over buffers)	56ft 4¾in	226mm	116.3mm	395.8mm
Height (over chimney)	13ft 3½in	53.2mm	27.3mm	93.1mm
Width (over cranks)	8ft 9½in	35.6mm	18.3mm	62.3mm
Wheel diameter (driving)	6ft 8½in	27.2mm	14mm	47.6mm
Wheel diameter (bogie)	3ft 8in	15.2mm	7.83mm	26.6mm
Wheel diameter (tender)	4ft 1½in	16.4mm	8.4mm	28.7mm
Cylinders (2)	18in by 26in	-	-	-

ABOVE: P. Chancellor/Colour Rail

NUMBERS AND BUILDS			
Engine Nos.	**Lot No.**	**Building dates**	**Works/Builder**
3405	N/a	1902	Swindon
3433-3442	141	1903	Swindon
3400-04/	127	1907-1908 (rebuilding)	Swindon
06-009			
Total: 20			

'City' liveries

1894-c1905

ABOVE: Colour Rail

C1905-1928

1928-1931

CAN I SEE ONE?

3441 *City of Winchester* became the first 'City' to be withdrawn (October 1927). The remaining 19 were all condemned between then and May 1931. The LNER offered *City of Truro* a home in its museum and York and the engine is, today, part of the National Collection. It is currently on display at STEAM–Museum of GWR at Swindon.

Available models

City of Truro became the second museum-quality model produced by Bachmann for the National Railway Museum. It was unveiled at the Gloucestershire Warwickshire Steam Railway in 2010, invited guests getting to enjoy a run behind the real thing.

Only available from the NRM, the models quickly sold out. It entered the main Branchline range in 2012, being offered as other 'Cities'. It's not currently in the Branchline range but, given its popularity, it will no doubt be back soon!

ABOVE: **Bachmann's 'OO' gauge 'City'.**

Detail differences

As built

A: Saturated boiler, short smokebox
B: Original chimney
C: Slide valves
D: Tall safety valve bonnet, no top feed
E: Original frames
F: No sandboxes
G: Porthole windows

RIGHT: Rail Archive Stephenson/Rail Online

Final condition

A: Superheated, with oil covers and extended smokebox
B: Later chimney
C: Piston valves (not visible)
D: Top feed
E: Sand boxes
F: Frame strengthening plates

RIGHT: C.A.J. Nevitt/ Rail Archive Stephenson/Rail Online

The Star 4-6-0

Designer	George Jackson Churchward
Lifespan	1907-1957
GWR power class	D (BR '5P')
GWR route restriction	Red

Railway modellers and enthusiasts we might be but who can deny that the sound of a loud and rumbly V8 engine doesn't stir the senses? The reason why automotive manufacturers opt for the 'Vee' configuration is that, by having two banks of cylinders, you can get effectively double the power of an in-line engine in the same space.

The same is true with steam locomotives. As the 19th century rolled into the 20th, locomotive engineers began to develop locomotives with more than two cylinders, for the simple reason that they generated more power. Compounding became a popular fad. This was where high pressure steam was used in one set of cylinders; as it lost pressure, it was used in a second set of low pressure cylinders.

Churchward liked the idea of a multi-cylinder version of his 'Saint' but didn't like the complexities of compounding. His solution? To create a four-cylinder locomotive.

That first attempt was 4-4-2 40. Its inside cylinders sat under the smokebox, with the outer ones in the more traditional place, obscuring the rear bogie wheel. Rocking levers kept the cylinders in sync with each other. However, there was no room between the frames for the Stephenson's valve gear that was used on the 'Saint' and so draughtsman W.H. Pearce designed a

version of Walschearts' gear. Known as the scissors gear, Churchward ordered it to be fitted to 40. It provoked the ire of the Midland Railway's Richard Deeley, who, simultaneously and independently of Pearce, had designed a very similar valve gear.

40 was built in 1906, about the time that Churchward settled on the 4-6-0 wheel arrangement. The first four-cylinder 4-6-0, the first of the 'Stars', appeared the following year. Much was copied from 40 but, aside from the additional driving wheel, the 'Stars' boasted conventional inside Walschearts' valve gear. It also had the Holcroft curved frames.

Legendary railway author O.S Nock called them "Celestial Stars" for very good reason. While the reputation of GWR locomotive development took a nose dive in the 1930s and '40s, it was at its zenith in the years either side of the First World War. Swindon craftsmanship couldn't be bettered, and the gradual replacement of coned and

half-coned boilers with taper boilers, the introduction of superheaters and de Glehn bogies made the best even better.

That quality came at a price. Churchward was asked by GWR management why it could only build two 'Stars' for the same money that the London & North Western

Railway was spending on three comparable locomotives. Churchward's response was typically blunt: "Because one of mine could pull two of their bloody things backwards."

It led to an exchange. 4005 *Polar Star* ran on the LNWR while 'Experiment' 4-6-0 1471 *Worcestershire* headed to the GWR. *Polar Star* quickly showed how advanced GWR design was. Churchward was vindicated while the LNWR was spurred to do better.

Further vindication came after the Second World War. The 'Castles' and 'Kings' started to suffer due to poor quality coal and reduced maintenance. They were cured by modifications to the superheaters and blastpipes. But the 'Stars' continued to perform much as they had in pre-war years, aided only by outside steampipes, inside steam pipes being the only flaw in Churchward's designs.

O.S. Nock continued to record superb performances up until the withdrawal of 4056 in 1957.

Below: **Churchward 'Star' 4014** *Knight of the Bath* **approaches Flax Bourton, just to the southwest of Bristol, with a Wolverhampton - Paignton express in 1939. Built in March 1908, the 4-6-0 was 31 years old and yet still capable, like so many of its classmates, of top-drawer performances. Sadly, it was condemned on June 4 1946.** C.R.L. Coles/Rail Archive Stephenson/Rail Online

'STAR' – KEY DIMENSIONS				
Dimensions	Prototype	1:76 scale	1:148 scale	1:43 scale
Length (over buffers)	64ft 1 ¾in	257.4mm	132.2mm	449.8mm
Height (over chimney)	13ft 3¼in	53.2mm	27.3mm	93.1mm
Width	8ft 11½in	36mm	18.5mm	63mm
Wheel diameter (driving)	6ft 8½in	27.2mm	14mm	47.6mm
Wheel diameter (bogie)	3ft 2in	12.8mm	6.5mm	22.4mm
Wheel diameter (tender)	4ft 1½in	16.4mm	8.44	28.7mm
Cylinders (4)	15in by 26in*	-	-	-
* Originally 14¼in by 26in				

NUMBERS AND BUILDS			
Engine Nos.	Lot No.	Building dates	Works
4001-10	168	1907	Swindon
4011-20	173	1908	Swindon
4021-30	178	1909	Swindon
4031-40	180	1910-11	Swindon
4041-45	195	1913	Swindon
4046-60	199	1914	Swindon
4061-72	217	1920-21	Swindon

WHERE WERE THEY SHEDDED?		
Shed name	GWR code	BR code
Bristol Bath Road	BRD	82A
Cardiff Canton*	CDF	86C
Cardiff East Dock	CED	88B
Carmarthen	CARM	87G
Chester West	CHR	84K
Exeter	EXE	83A
Gloucester Horton Road	GLO	83D
Hereford	SRD	84A
Llanelli	LLY	87F
Neath Court Sart	NEA	87A
Newton Abbot	NA	83A
Old Oak Common	PDN	81A
Oxford	OXF	81F
Penzance	PZ	83G
Plymouth Laira	LA	83D
Reading	RDG	81D
Shrewsbury	SALOP	84G
Swindon	SDN	82C
Swansea Landore	LDR	87E
Taunton	TB	83B
Truro	TR	83F
Tyseley	TYS	84E
Westbury	WES	82D
Wolverhampton Oxley	OXY	84B
Wolverhampton Stafford Road	SRD	84A
Worcester	WOS	85A
Weymouth Radipole	WEY	82F

'Star' tenders

Churchward 3,500gal (short tender)

Churchward 3,500gal (long fender)

Collett 4,000gal

RIGHT: Trevor Owen/Colour Rail

CAN I SEE ONE?

The 'Stars' were withdrawn between 1932 and 1957 (not including those rebuilt as 'Castles' - p28). However, 4003 *Lode Star* was selected for official preservation in 1951 and shares its time between the National Railway Museum, York and STEAM at Swindon.

Model timeline

2013: This is quite a short timeline: Hornby introduced the only ready-to-run 'Star' in all three popular scales – other than museum-quality brass models in 'O'. It's been in and out of the catalogue over the years but is not in 2025's range.

Hornby's 'OO' gauge 'Star'

Detail differences

ABOVE: Rail Archive Stephenson/Rail Online

Early 'Star'

A: 4001-4010 fitted with small chimneys from new; replaced after a couple of years
B: Solid slidebars from 4003 onwards
C: De Glehn bogie from 4011
D: 4002/08-09/11-16/18 were fitted with front footsteps for a couple of years (dates unclear)
E: Automatic Train Control introduced in 1908; widespread fitment between 1923-27
F: Bogie brakes removed from 1923

ABOVE: F.H. Stingemore/Rail Archive Stephenson/Rail Online

Mid-life 'Star'

A: Fluted inside front cylinder cover (from 4021 onwards)
B: Superheater cover (from 4021; all later converted)
C: Top feed (from 4041, later all engines)
D: Solid cab footsteps (from 4021 onwards)
E: Porthole windows covered circa 1924

Final condition 'Star' – 1

A: Reversing gear cover added during Second World War
B: Speedometers fitted from 1937 (selected engines)
C: Beading removed from 4061 onwards, later all engines
D: Whistle shields fitted circa 1927
E: Short safety valve bonnet from 1927 onwards
F: Cast iron chimney (introduced from 4061 onwards)
G: Top lamp iron moved to smokebox from 1932

BELOW: Trevor Owen/Colour Rail

Final condition 'Star' – 2

A: Outside steam pipes ('Castle' or 'elbow' style) fitted from 1929
B: Four-cone ejector (from 4046 onwards, later all engines)
C: Fluted coupling rods fitted to (4061/62/67-72) for short period; dates difficult to ascertain
D: 15in cylinders (from 4041)

ABOVE: Colour Rail

KEY Publishing — Model World SHOP

EXCLUSIVE SIGNALBOX KITS

Take control of your trains with PJM Models laser-cut signalbox kits

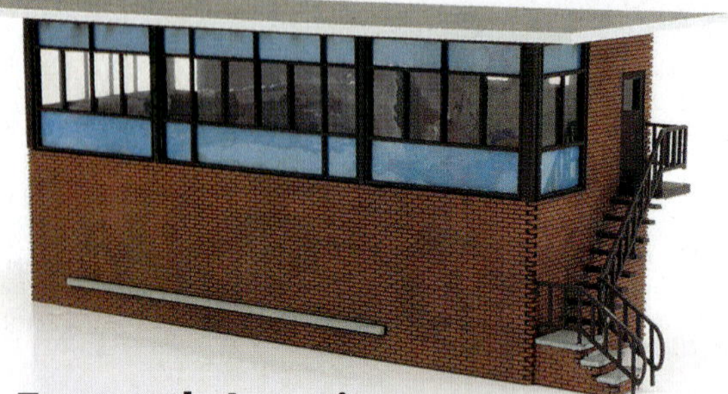

Exmouth Junction signalbox for 'OO' gauge

Cat No: MOD147

Price: £32.99

Helpston signalbox for 'OO' gauge

Cat No: MOD125

Price: £32.99

Yarnton signalbox for 'OO' gauge

Cat No: PJM170

Price: £32.99

NEW

Crewe Station A 'box for 'OO' gauge

Cat No: PJM200

Price: £19.99

Norton Bridge signalbox for 'OO' gauge

Cat No: MOD71

Price: £47.99

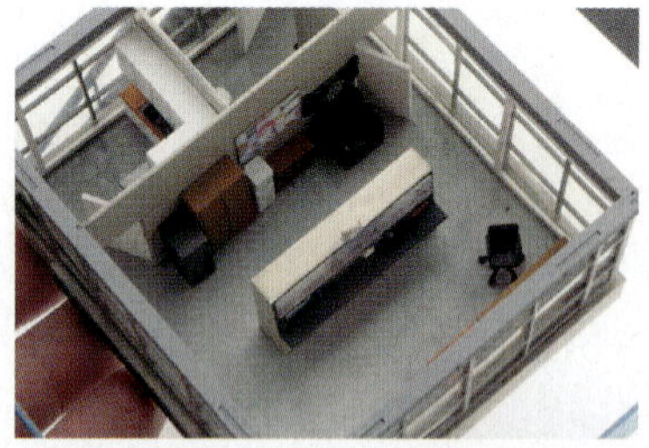

Norton Bridge interior kit for 'OO' gauge

Cat No: MOD78

Price: £12.99

CHECK OUT OUR FULL COLLECTION OF MODELS HERE:

keymodelworld.com/shop

910/25

The French engines

Designer	See text
Lifespan	1903-1920s
GWR power class	N/a
GWR route restriction	N/a

ABOVE: **102 *La France*, photographed circa 1904. The locomotive was delivered in a black livery with the GWR emblems on the leading splashers. It was coupled to a short fender GWR tender on arrival in the UK. GWR enginemen were very proud of the French trio.** Rail Archive Stephenson/Rail Online

How do you know you're the best? By beating the best!

Churchward was not the only railway engineer experimenting and developing new ideas around the turn of the 20th century.

Alfred de Glehn's name might sound French but he was born in England in 1848 to a German father and a Scottish mother. He later moved to France, changing his name from von Glehn to something more Gallic. Working at the locomotive builder Société Alsacienne de Constructions Mécaniques, he began to perfect compounding, alongside Gaston du Bousquet, chief engineer of the Chemins de Fer du Nord.

Compounding is the process whereby steam is first used in high pressure cylinders and then used again in low pressure cylinders. Some British engineers became enamoured with compounding while others, Churchward included, thought it was an over complicated system.

But as Churchward was working on 100, the de Glehn compounds were catching the eye, becoming the machines against which all others were judged. If Churchward wanted to design the best, he had to build something

better than the de Glehn engines – and in order to find out what that required, there had to be a direct comparison.

So the GWR placed an order with SACM at Belfort, close to the Swiss border, for a locomotive. Aside from being scaled to fit the GWR loading gauge, fitted with GWR buffing gear and vacuum brakes and having GWR profile tyres, it was the same as the engines doing the sterling work on the Nord.

The GWR's new 102 *La France* arrived in 1903 and was pitted against the third new 4-6-0, 171 (p27). There were two key differences. The French engine was a 4-4-2 and the boiler pressure was 227lb/sq in. So, 171's boiler pressure was increased from 200lb/sq in to 225lb/sq in. Then, in 1904, it was rebuilt as a 4-4-2.

It quickly became clear that while 102 put in some superb performances on the GWR, 171 – now named *Albion* – was very much its equal.

The power output was broadly similar and while the French engine did consume less coal, it wasn't enough to convince Churchward to adopt compounding.

To be absolutely certain, two more French engines arrived in 1905. 103 and 104 were larger than 102, a key giveaway being the side window cabs. They also had inside bearing bogies.

Again, coal consumption was roughly on par with the GWR engines. Oil consumption was higher on the French engines but what impressed most was their build quality, the mileages they were running between shopping and their overall smoothness.

It's impossible to understate how important these engines were to the GWR achieving the success it did with locomotive design from 1903 until 1927. Swindon Works upped its workmanship. The inside bearing bogie was adopted as the GWR standard.

But the most significant change to Churchward's thinking was to design a four-cylinder locomotive. And that became 40, the forerunner of the 'Stars'.

It was the greater adhesion offered by a six-coupled engine that finally convinced Churchward to adopt the 4-6-0 wheel arrangement… and thus the die was cast for the GWR to produce the superlative designs it did.

As for the French trio, they were later fitted with GWR No. 1 boilers and would serve the Great Western Railway until the late 1920s.

102 – KEY DIMENSIONS				
Dimensions	Prototype	1:76 scale	1:148 scale	1:43 scale
Length (over buffers)	63ft ¾in	252.6mm	129.7mm	441.4mm
Height	N/a	N/a	N/a	N/a
Width	N/a	N/a	N/a	N/a
Wheel diameter (driving)	6ft 8½in	27.2mm	14mm	47.6mm
Wheel diameter (bogie)	2ft 11⅞in	12mm	6mm	21mm
Wheel diameter (trailing)	4ft 7⅞in	19.2mm	9.8mm	33.6mm
Wheel diameter (tender)	4ft 1½in	16.4mm	8.4mm	28.7mm
Cylinders (HPx2)	N/a	-	-	-
Cylinders (LPx2)	N/a	-	-	-

Rail Archive Stephenson/Rail Online

103/104 – KEY DIMENSIONS				
Dimensions	Prototype	1:76 scale	1:148 scale	1:43 scale
Length (over buffers)	63ft 7¼in	255.4mm	131.1mm	446.3mm
Height	N/a	N/a	N/a	N/a
Width	N/a	N/a	N/a	N/a
Wheel diameter (driving)	6ft 8½in	27.2mm	14mm	47.6mm
Wheel diameter (bogie)	3ft 2in	12.8mm	6.5mm	22.4mm
Wheel diameter (trailing)	3ft 8in	15.2mm	7.83mm	26.6mm
Wheel diameter (tender)	4ft 1½in	16.4mm	8.4mm	28.7mm
Cylinders (HPx2)	14³⁄₁₆in by 25³⁄₁₆in	-	-	-
(LPx2)	23⅝in by 25³⁄₁₆in	-	-	-

NUMBERS AND BUILDS			
Engine Nos.	Lot No.	Building dates	Works/ Builder
102	146	1902	SACN, France
103-104	157	1905	SACN, France
Total: 3			

Below: Rail Archive Stephenson/Rail Online

ABOVE: **De Glehn 4-4-2 104 in almost original condition.** Rail Archive Stephenson/Rail Online

ABOVE: **Between 1914 and 1916, the French trio were rebuilt with GWR standard boilers, complete with top feed. These required large outside steampipes to be fitted. This didn't improve the looks, as this portrait of 104, now named *Alliance*, shows.** W.H. Whitworth/Rail Archive Stephenson/Rail Online

The Great Bear

One wonders what it must have been like to see *The Great Bear* for the first time. This chap looks impressed, despite the fact that the engine was nearing the end of its days when photographed inside Old Oak Common shed on May 21 1921. Norman Preedy Collection/Rail Photoprints

Designer	George Jackson Churchward
Lifespan	1908-1924
GWR power class	N/a
GWR route restriction	Special Red

The GWR was not known for its subtlety. Having trounced the LNER during the 1925 exchanges, 4079 *Pendennis Castle* was displayed at the 1925 Wembley Exhibition a few weeks later with a sign proudly proclaiming it to be Britain's most powerful express locomotive.

Then, in July, the GWR sent two 'Castles' to the North East, to take part in the celebrations organised by the LNER to mark 100 years since the Stockton & Darlington Railway opened. This event is widely seen as the birth of the modern railway and the LNER, which now owned the former S&D route, took its responsibilities to honour railway history very seriously.

Of those 'Castles', 4082 *Windsor Castle* was an obvious choice. It was the GWR's 'Royal' engine and hauled its royal train as exhibit No. 50 during the cavalcade on July 2 1925.

The other train that the GWR chose to display at the event was its new rake of articulated coaches. To haul these vehicles, the GWR could have sent any 'Castle' (4079 excepted – it was still at Wembley).

But it chose 111 *Viscount Churchill*. Gresley 'A1' 4-6-2 2563 *William Whitelaw* (Exhibit 30), represented the zenith of LNER locomotive development while Raven 'A2' 4-6-2 2400 *City of Newcastle* was entrusted in hauling the LNER's most modern coaches.

The message was simple: in sending 111, the GWR was reminding visitors that it had built Britain's first 4-6-2.

And while 111 might have looked like a 'Castle', it still contained some parts – as well as its number – from the GWR's only 4-6-2, *The Great Bear*.

Churchward had proven that 'big' was the way forward when it came to locomotive design. 100 (p25) was larger than anything else around at the time. Then came the 'Stars' and, by the time he retired at the end of 1921, he'd already designed the mighty '47XX' 2-8-0, ruling out a large-boilered 4-8-0 as it was a bit too big.

While successor Collett would go on to prove that the 'Star' could be increased in size (the 'Castle' and the 'King'), Churchward decided that a 4-6-2 offered a suitable platform for a big express engine.

The frames, cylinders and motion were based on the 'Star', although the frames were extended at the rear for the radial truck, which, unlike later 'Pacifics', had inside bearings.

The boiler was a whopper. The No. 1 was 14ft 10in long and increased in diameter from 4ft 11in to 5ft 6in. By contrast, the new No. 6 boiler was 23ft long and increased in diameter from 5ft 6in to 6ft. The firebox was equally mammoth and, being wide with a sloping backplate, was a radical departure from the GWR standard. Churchward even penned a new eight-wheel bogie tender to complement the new locomotive.

Sadly, *The Great Bear* was perhaps too big. It was limited to running between London and Bristol and those inside bearings would plague it. Indeed, when learning of Nigel Gresley's quest to design a 'Pacific', Churchward apparently said that the GWR could simply have sold him *The Great Bear*.

The result of Gresley's labours was the 'A1' and controversy still rages that his successor, Edward Thompson, rebuilt the first one, butchering its handsome lines.

But, here again, the GWR was first. Despite being something of a white elephant, *The Great Bear* was still held in high regard at Swindon, except, that is, by Charles Collett. He quickly had it rebuilt as a 'Castle' in 1924.

Whereas Thompson kept the name *Great Northern* for 'A1/1' 4-6-2 113 (BR 60113), Collett didn't even do that. Only the number survived and a few parts served as a reminder that the GWR was a pioneer.

Dimensions	Prototype	1:76 scale	1:148 scale	1:43 scale
Length (over buffers)	70ft 10¾in	284mm	146mm	497mm
Height	N/a	N/a	N/a	N/a
Width	N/a	N/a	N/a	N/a
Wheel diameter (driving)	6ft 8½in	27.2mm	14mm	47.6mm
Wheel diameter (bogie)	3ft 2in	12.8mm	6.5mm	22.4mm
Wheel diameter (trailing)	3ft 8in	15.2mm	7.83mm	26.6mm
Wheel diameter (tender)	3ft 2in	12.8mm	6.5mm	22.4mm
Cylinders (4)	15in by 26in	-	-	-

ABOVE: STEAM Picture Library

The Great Bear liveries

1908-1924

NUMBERS AND BUILDS

Engine Nos.	Lot No.	Building dates	Works/Builder
111	171	1908	Swindon
Total: 1			

CAN I SEE ONE?

The Great Bear was rebuilt at Swindon in 1924, returning to service as 'Castle' 111 *Viscount Portal*. It was one of the first 'Castles' to be withdrawn, although not the first as three rebuilt 'Stars' preceded it. However, it was condemned on July 13 1953 and was scrapped three months later.

The Great Bear – almost original condition

A: Front footsteps removed shortly after entering service
B: Three row superheater
C: No top feed

Available models

Sadly, no ready-to-run models of *The Great Bear* have been offered and what kits have been produced are fairly thin on the ground these days, regardless of scale.

ABOVE: Robert Brookman/Rail Archive Stephenson/Rail Online

The Great Bear – final condition

A: Top feed fitted (from 1913)
B: Two-row superheater fitted (from 1913)
C: Four-cone ejector added (1920)
D: Cast iron chimney fitted (1920)

ABOVE: Rail Archive Stephenson/Rail Online

The 'Hall' 4-6-0

Designer	Charles Collett
Lifespan	1924-1965
GWR power class	D (BR '5MT')
GWR route restriction	Red

What's the world's most famous locomotive? *Flying Scotsman*, surely? Stephenson's *Rocket*? Or is it *Thomas The Tank Engine*?

One contender has to be 5972 *Hogwarts Castle*.

Bulleid 'West Country' 34027 *Taw Valley* was the first locomotive to carry the distinctive red livery of Hogwarts Railways. It was repainted in 2000 as part of the promotion for J.K. Rowling's book series about a school for witches and wizards but was not chosen to star in the subsequent films because it apparently looked too modern.

The slightly antiquated shape of a Great Western Railway better suited the producers' needs… and 5972 *Olton Hall* has cemented its place in cinematic history.

The *Harry Potter* film franchise is now considered to be in the same league as *Star Wars* or *James Bond* and *Olton Hall* is viewed by up to 6,000 people a day at the Studio Tour London – The Making of Harry Potter exhibition in Hertfordshire.

You'd be amazed at how much locomotive-shaped merchandise is available with 5972 on the side. Universal Studios, in Florida, has built an electrically operated people mover shaped like 5972. And in the most bizarre move, 4920 *Dumbleton Hall*, is now on display at The Making of *Harry Potter* in Japan!

ABOVE: **The ultimate go-anywhere, do-anything machine… oh, were you thinking we were talking about the Brush Type 4? D1709 might represent the new era under the fabulous trainshed at Paddington on April 3 1964, but 'Hall' 6937 *Conyngham Hall* is every bit as versatile as this diesel interloper, having just arrived with the 4.33pm from Weston-Super-Mare.** Brian Stephenson/Rail Online

Did Charles Collett ever imagine such a scenario in the early 1920s when the GWR's running department made an approach for an improved '43XX' 2-6-0?

The GWR helped pioneer the concept of the 'mixed traffic' locomotive, one that was equally at home on passenger or goods trains. In fact, this had only happened by accident. Harold Holcroft, inspired by a fact-finding trip to North America, suggested to Churchward that a 2-6-0 ought to be added to the range of standard engines and Churchward told him to design one. The resulting '43XX' was an inspired addition, proving its worth on secondary and lighter goods duties.

The problem with the class was that they were often called on to work trains far in excess of their capacity. They also lost stability at higher speeds.

Churchward had given designing a larger '43XX' some attention, but it fell to successor Charles Collett to devise a solution. And it was a moment of genius. Rather than spend time and effort on a new design, Collett decided that a 'Saint' with smaller wheels would do the trick and so, once the drawing office had finished preparing a diagram, 'Saint' 2925 *Saint Martin* was brought into Swindon for rebuilding. It returned to service in 1924 with new 6ft diameter driving wheels and a larger cab.

The first production 'Halls' began to emerge from Swindon in 1928 and while *Saint Martin* was often considered the first of the class, there were some important changes between it and the production engines. This was because the production engines were designed with 6ft wheels from the outset, so the bogie wheels were 3ft diameter and the boiler pitched slightly higher.

The 'Halls' served the Western Region until the end of steam in December 1965. But the class left an important legacy: William Stanier used it as inspiration for his 'Black Five', the ultimate mixed traffic engine that brought down the curtain on main line steam in Britain on August 11 1968.

HALL - KEY DIMENSIONS				
Dimensions	Prototype	1:76 scale	1:148 scale	1:43 scale
Length (over buffers)	63ft ¼in	252.6mm	129.7mm	441.4mm
Height (over chimney)	13ft 3¼in	53.3mm	27.3mm	93.1mm
Width (over cylinders)	8ft 11¼in	36mm	18.5mm	63mm
Wheel diameter (driving)	6ft 0in	24mm	12.3mm	42mm
Wheel diameter (bogie)	3ft 0in	12mm	6.1mm	21mm
Wheel diameter (tender)	4ft 1½in	16.4mm	8.4mm	28.7mm
Cylinders (2)	18in by 30in	N/a	N/a	N/a

NUMBERS AND BUILDS			
Engine Nos.	Lot No.	Building dates	Works/ Builder
4900	N/a	1924	Swindon
4901-4980	254	1928-1930	Swindon
4981-5900	268	1930-1931	Swindon
5901-5920	275	1931	Swindon
5921-5940	281	1933	Swindon
5941-5950	290	1935	Swindon
5951-5965	297	1935-36	Swindon
5966-5975	304	1937	Swindon
5976-5985	311	1938	Swindon
5986-5995	327	1939-1940	Swindon
5996-6905	333	1940	Swindon
6906-6915	338	1940-1941	Swindon
6916-6958	340	1941-1943	Swindon
Total: 258			

CAN I SEE ONE?

The first 'Hall' to be withdrawn was 4911 *Bowden Hall* destroyed by German bombs during the Second World War. Production 'Halls' were withdrawn between 1960 and 1965. Ten survive: 4920 *Dumbleton Hall* (see text), 4930 *Hagley Hall* (Severn Valley Railway), 4936 *Kinlet Hall* (Tyseley Locomotive Works), 4953 *Pitchford Hall* (Epping Ongar Railway), 4965 *Rood Ashton Hall* (Tyseley Locomotive Works), 4979 *Wootton Hall* (Ribble Steam Railway), 5900 *Hinderton Hall* (Didcot Railway Centre), 5952 *Cogan Hall* (Tyseley Locomotive Works), 5967 *Bickmarsh Hall* (Llangollen Railway) and 5972 *Olton Hall* (see text).

WHERE WERE THEY SHEDDED?		
Shed name	GWR code	BR code
Banbury	BAN	84C
Basingstoke	BAS	-
Bristol Bath Road	BRD	82A
Bristol St Philips Marsh	SPM	82B
Bristol Barrow Road		82E*
Cardiff Canton*	CDF	86C
Cardiff East Dock	CED	88B
Carmarthen	CARM	87G
Chester West	CHR	84K
Croes Newydd	CNYD	84J
		89B (1960-1963)
		6C (1963-1967)
Didcot	DID	81E
Duffryn Yard	DYD	87B
Ebbw Junction	NA	83A
Exeter	EXE	83A
Fishguard Goodwick	FDG	81A
Gloucester Horton Road	GLO	83D
Hereford	SRD	84A
Leamington	LMTN	84D
Llanelli	LLY	87F
Neath Court Sart	NEA	87A
Newton Abbot	NA	83A

(CONT'D)		
Shed name	GWR code	BR code
Neyland	NEY	87H
Old Oak Common	PDN	81A
Oxford	OXF	81F
Penzance	PZ	83G
		84D
Plymouth Laira	LA	83D
Pontypool Road	PPRD	86G
Reading	RDG	81D
Severn Tunnel Junction	STJ	86E
Shrewsbury	SALOP	84G
Southall	SHL	81C
St Blazey	SBZ	83E
Stourbridge Junction	STB	84F
Swindon	SDN	82C
Swansea Landore	LDR	87E
Taunton	TB	83B
Truro	TR	83F
Tyseley	TYS	84E
Westbury	WES	82D
Weymouth Radipole	WEY	82F
Wolverhampton Oxley	OXY	84B
Wolverhampton Stafford Road	SRD	84A
Worcester	WOS	85A
* London Midland Region shed until 1958		

'Hall' liveries

1928-1934

1934-1940

1940-1947

ABOVE: Trevor Owen/Colour Rail

1948-56

Circa 1956

1956-1965

'Hall' tenders

Churchward 3,500gal (long fender)

Collett 3,500gal

Collett 4,000gal

Hawksworth 4,000gal

Model timeline

1980   Two models are available – Hornby's 'OO' gauge model and the Graham Farish 'N' gauge example. However, the standard of either is not high. Hornby retired the former Tri-ang 'Hall' tooling, which dated from 1966, in 1983.

2003   The old Farish 'N' gauge 'Hall' is re-introduced by Bachmann under its 'Graham Farish by Bachmann' brand. It's last produced circa 2008.

2005   Bachmann Branchline introduces new 'OO' gauge 'Hall'. It was originally intended to be a 'Grange' but was switched to a 'Hall' to avoid duplication with Hornby's.

2011   Dapol produces new 'N' gauge 'Hall'.

2015   Hornby made a surprise announcement when it unveiled a new 'OO' gauge 'Hall' under its Railroad brand. It was a high-fidelity model where the quality of the finish is below the full-range standard.

Models available

Branchline 32-002: 4953 *Pitchford Hall*, BR lined black
Branchline 32-004A: 5900 *Hinderton Hall*, GWR green
Branchline 32-008: 4936 *Kinlet Hall*, BR lined green
RRP: £189.95. Availability: Bachmann Branchline stockists

STOP PRESS: Graham Farish has just announced all-new 'Halls' and 'Modified Halls' in 'N'. See Hornby Magazine for more.

Hornby's 'OO' gauge 'Hall' is not in its 2025 catalogue…

…and neither is Dapol's 'N' gauge model.

Detail differences

4900

A: Boiler is pitched at (8ft 1¾in) compared to 8ft 6in of production 'Hall'
B: Bogie wheel is 3ft 2in diameter; 3ft 0in on production 'Hall'
C: Outside steam pipes fitted in December 1948'

RIGHT: Rail Photoprints Collection

Early condition 'Hall'

A: Front valve spindle crosshead guides (4901-40/51-77)
B: Spring compensating beams (4901-80)

RIGHT: Ray Hinton Collection/Rail Photoprints

Chimneys

Standard 'Hall' chimney

Narrower 'Grange' chimney

'ID' chimney

Automatic Train Control

New from 4921; older engines retro-fitted

Fire iron tunnels

4901-5921: not fitted

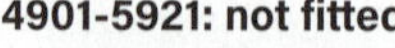

Fitted to 5922 onwards

Cabside handrail

Straight type: 4901-5920

Twin type: 5921-5975

ABOVE: Trevor Owen/Colour Rail

Curved type: 5976-6958

Top lamp iron

4901-5921

5922 onwards; later changed on earlier engines

ABOVE: The 'County' 4-4-0s were not the most successful of Churchward's designs, they were still a handsome looking machine. That said, there was something North American about the gap between the bogie and driving wheels. 3818 *County of Radnor* passes Kensal Green gasworks in August 1931, with a Down semi-fast working. George R. Grigs/Rail Archive Stephenson/Rail Online

Designer	George Jackson Churchward
Lifespan	1904-1933
GWR power class	C
GWR route restriction	Red

Churchward almost had a touch of Croesus about him - every locomotive design he touched, he seemed to strike gold. Even his so-called improvements turned gold into, well, better gold. Take the '44XX' 2-6-2Ts for example. Fitting them with larger wheels created the superlative '45XX'.

Yet he didn't always get it right, particularly in the early years when he was still experimenting. Take the 'Kruger' 2-6-0 for example. But he did suffer from one or two failures later on in his career, too. And this was one of them.

There were six designs on Churchward's initial list of standard locomotives: a 4-6-0 with 6ft 8½in driving wheels, one with 5ft 8in wheels, a 2-8-0, a 2-6-2T with 5ft 8in wheels and two four-coupled engines, one a 4-4-0 and the other a 4-4-2T, both with 6ft 8½in wheels.

As you can see on p47, there were myriad Dean-Churchward 'double frame' 4-4-0s that were perfectly suited to handling secondary passenger duties. But, as there was a 4-4-0 on his list, Churchward built one. The class became known as 'Counties' as they were all named after English, Welsh and Irish counties.

These engines were effectively 'Saints' minus the rear set of driving wheels. They used the No. 4 boiler. Churchward must have felt confident that combining these now proven standard parts would work together,

The 'County' 4-4-0

for an order was placed for ten, straight off the drawing board.

He only made that choice three times – the others were the 4-4-2Ts, known as 'County Tanks' and the '43XXs'. For every other standard design, a prototype was ordered first.

Harold Holcroft, in *An Outline of G.W. Locomotive Practice, 1837-1947*, wonders why the 'Counties' were built, particularly as new double-frame 4-4-0s were being built concurrently. He points out that the only difference – frames aside - between the 'Counties' and the 'Cities' was a 4in difference in the cylinder stroke.

"The inside cylinders and shorter stroke gave a better and more comfortable riding engine at speed," he says.

The short wheelbase and big cylinders on the 'County' produced an engine that rolled and oscillated. They soon gained the nickname 'Churchward's Rough Riders'. And yet whereas only 20 'Cities' were built, more and more 'Rough Riders' continued to emerge from Swindon Works.

Sir William Stanier offers a different perspective. As the London & North Western Railway's Francis Webb wouldn't permit 4-6-0s on the LNWR/GWR Joint railway between Shrewsbury and Hereford. Stanier says: "Churchward was not going to be instructed by Webb," and so designed an engine offering too much power.

The final batch of ten was built in 1911-12, which was another odd decision considering that Swindon was also building more two-

cylinder and four-cylinder 4-6-0s, not to mention the more useful '43XX' 2-6-0s.

This batch had some differences. Firstly, they had the Holcroft curves, whereas previous engines had the straight frames of the early 'Saints', plus superheated boilers with extended smokeboxes (a feature gradually fitted to the early builds). The last batch also had screw reversers rather than a lever reverser and the cylinder centre line was 2½in lower.

Holcroft summed up the class succinctly, calling it "an assembly of standard parts for the sake of standardisation". He's not wrong when he called it "the least successful of the Churchward designs".

These disappeared swiftly, too - withdrawals started in 1930 and all had gone by the end of 1933.

Dimensions	Prototype	1:76 scale	1:148 scale	1:43 scale
Length (over buffers)	57ft 10¾in	229mm	117.5mm	400mm
Height (over chimney)	13ft 3¼in	53.3mm	27.3mm	93.1mm
Width (over cylinders)	8ft 11in	35.2mm	18.1mm	61.6mm
Wheel diameter (driving)	6ft 8½in	27.2mm	14mm	47.6mm
Wheel diameter (bogie)	3ft 2in	12.8mm	6.5mm	22.4mm
Wheel diameter (tender)	4ft 1½in	16.4mm	8.4mm	28.7mm
Cylinders (2)	18in by 30in	-	-	-

Rail Archive Stephenson/Rail Online

NUMBERS AND BUILDS			
Engine Nos.	Lot No.	Building dates	Works/Builder
3473-3482*	149	1904	Swindon
3801-3820	165	1906	Swindon
3821-3830	184	1911-12	Swindon
Total: 40			
* 3473 later became 3800; 3474-3482 became 3831-3840			

CAN I SEE ONE?

The last 'County' 4-4-0, 3834 *County of Somerset*, was withdrawn in November 1933. The 41st 'County', 3840 *County of Montgomery*, is being built at Tyseley Locomotive Works by the Churchward County Trust, using a genuine No. 4 boiler.

'County' liveries

1902-c1905

ABOVE: Colour Rail

C1905-1928

1928-1934

Available models

Hornby introduced four new 'OO' gauge outside cylinder 4-4-0 models in 1981, one for each of the 'Big Four'. Outwardly, they captured the character of the prototype but they all shared the same chassis and so there was some stretching of dimensions to fit.

For the GWR, the only outside cylinder 4-4-0 Hornby could choose was the 'County'. It was a typical Hornby product of the time, with the tender-mounted Ringfield motor.

Retired in the 1990s, Hornby refreshed the model circa 2011, fitting it with locomotive-drive and a DCC socket. It reappeared under the Railroad banner and makes frequent returns to the catalogue, although isn't in the 2025 range.

Detail differences

LEFT: Colour Rail

Almost original condition – 1

A: Saturated boiler with short smokebox
B: Later cast iron chimney
C: Top feed (fitted 1911 onwards)
D: Front straight frames
E: Outside mounted sandboxes (3820 onwards)
F: Inside brake rigging (3820 onwards)
G: Straight rear frames and steps

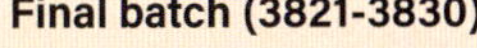

LEFT: Colour Rail

Almost original condition – 2

A: High cylinder line
B: Superheated boiler with extended smokebox
C: Lever reverser

LEFT: Colour Rail

Final batch (3821-3830)

A: Curved front frame
B: Screw reverser
C: Curved rear frame
D: Low cylinder line

Designer	Charles Collett
Lifespan	1936-1965
GWR power class	D (BR '5MT')
GWR route restriction	Red

GWR fireman-cum-author Harold Gasson recounts a story in his book *Nostalgic Days* whereby an inspector was asked what his favourite locomotives were. The inspector's audience expected to hear a discourse on the merits of the 'King' versus the 'Castle'. What they got was a surprise: the mighty '47XX' 2-8-0... and the Collett 'Grange'.

Gasson waxes lyrical about the 'Grange' in his first book, *Footplate Days*. "One of the most loved engines on the Great Western" is how he describes them. "They had a gentleness about them, a tolerance and an air of tranquillity that would forgive any transgression on the part of a ham-fisted driver or inexperienced fireman."

He added that "this gentleness could be deceptive as when the time came to move, the 'Grange' could react with an aggression", describing how its 5ft 8in driving wheels would "attack".

This was a view echoed by amateur-engineman and GWR enthusiast Kenneth Leech as well as Tyseley footplateman Dick Potts. Leech recalled a trip on 6859 *Yiewsley Grange* where the engine emerged from Box Tunnel at 85mph, 10mph over the speed limit. Potts tells of 6845 *Paviland Grange* apparently topping 90mph on the approach to Leamington in an attempt to make up time; apparently the engine was going so fast that "vibration ceased and we seemed to be floating."

The key to the class's success was those 5ft 8in driving wheels.

The 'Grange' was developed as a way of replacing those elderly Dean and Churchward era 4-4-0s (p27) as well as older Churchward '43XX' 2-6-0s. However, the GWR was thrifty if nothing else and decided to re-use the '43XX's' 5ft 8in driving wheels on the new engines. Essentially, the 'Grange' was a 'Hall' with smaller wheels but that small change made a world of difference.

The 'Grange', according to Gasson, "had the edge over the 'Hall' for all-out power," and to see the dip of the frame behind the cylinder "brought a feeling of joy in my heart." The 'Hall' could be greedy on coal but not so the 'Grange'.

It's perhaps sad that the 'Grange' was only considered a rebuild of the '43XXs'

because production was curtailed by the Second World War. It never re-started and the proposed 6880-6899 were never built. However, Churchward's 'Moguls' continued to serve until the end of Western Region steam while 'Hall' production continued through the war years and into the 1950s.

That interchangeability of parts meant that 'Granges' would often emerge from Swindon Works with 'Hall' boilers, the higher superheat version or improved draughting making a great engine even better.

No two-cylinder GWR 4-6-0 was included on the list of locomotives destined to officially preserved and so the Great Western Society decided to save one. It's one of the great ironies that while it considered saving a 'Grange', it opted for 'Modified Hall' 6998 *Burton Agnes Hall* instead. Woodham Brothers bought 17 'Halls' and 'Modified Halls' and all would be saved for preservation; in the event, the last 'Granges' were withdrawn at by the end of 1965 and all 80 scrapped.

Happily, a group of enthusiasts were determined not to let the 'Grange' reputation die and set about creating a new one. The 81st 'Grange', 6880 *Betton Grange*, finally entered service in 2024.

The 'Granges' served the Western Region until the end of 1965, the last full year of steam on the region. Many of the last survivors ended up in terrible external condition, missing name, cabside and smokebox plates, yet they were still capable of putting in superb performances, as illustrated by 6848 *Toddington Grange* blasting away from Banbury with the 10.08am York-Bournemouth on March 27 1965. Brian Stephenson/Rail Online

The 'Grange' 4-6-0

Dimensions	Prototype	1:76 scale	1:148 scale	1:43 scale
Length (over buffers)	63ft ¼in	252.6mm	129.7mm	441.4mm
Height (over chimney)	12 10½in	48.5mm	24.9mm	84.7mm
Width (over cylinders)	8ft 11¼in	36mm	18.5mm	63mm
Wheel diameter (driving)	5ft 8in	23.2mm	11.9mm	40.6mm
Wheel diameter (bogie)	3ft 0in	12mm	6.1mm	21mm
Wheel diameter (tender)	4ft 1½in	16.4mm	8.4mm	28.7mm
Cylinders (2)	18½in by 30in	-	-	-

ABOVE: STEAM Picture Library

NUMBERS AND BUILDS

Engine Nos.	Lot No.	Building dates	Works/ Builder
6800-99	308	1936-1939	Swindon
Total: 80			

CAN I SEE ONE?

The final four 'Granges' – 6847-49/72 – were withdrawn in December 1965 and the whole class scrapped. However, the 81st 'Grange', 6880 *Betton Grange*, entered service in 2024. It used the boiler from 'Modified Hall' 7927 *Willington Hall* and the bogie from 'Hall' 5952 *Cogan Hall* but the rest is new. It's normally based at the Gloucestershire Warwickshire Steam Railway.

WHERE WERE THEY SHEDDED?

Shed name	GWR code	BR code
Banbury	BAN	84C
Birkenhead Mollington Street	BHD	-
Bristol St Philips Marsh	SPM	82B
Bristol Barrow Road		82E*
Cardiff Canton	CDF	86C
Cardiff East Dock	CED	88B
Carmarthen	CARM	87G
Chester West	CHR	84K
Croes Newydd	CNYD	84J
		89B (1960-1963)
		6C (1963-1967)
Didcot	DID	81E
Ebbw Junction	NA	83A
Exeter	EXE	83A
Fishguard Goodwick	FDG	81A
Gloucester Horton Road	GLO	83D
Hereford	SRD	84A
Kidderminster	KDR	85D
Leamington	LMTN	84D
Llanelli	LLY	87F
Neath Court Sart	NEA	87A
Newton Abbot	NA	83A
Neyland	NEY	87H

(CONT'D)		
Shed name	GWR code	BR code
Old Oak Common	PDN	81A
Oxford	OXF	81F
Penzance	PZ	83G
		84D
Plymouth Laira	LA	83D
Pontypool Road	PPRD	86G
Radyr	RYR	88A
Reading	RDG	81D
Severn Tunnel Junction	STJ	86E
Southall	SHL	81C
St Blazey	SBZ	83E
Stourbridge Junction	STB	84F
Swindon	SDN	82C
Swansea Landore	LDR	87E
Taunton	TB	83B
Truro	TR	83F
Tyseley	TYS	84E
Westbury	WES	82D
Weymouth Radipole	WEY	82F
Wolverhampton Oxley	OXY	84B
Wolverhampton Stafford Road	SRD	84A
Worcester	WOS	85A
* London Midland Region shed until 1958		

'Grange' liveries

1934-1940 **1940-1947** **1950-1956** **Circa 1956** **1956-1965**

'Grange' tenders

Churchward 3,500gal (long fender) **Collett 3,500gal** **Collett 4,000gal**

Model timeline

2005   Both Hornby and Bachmann Branchline announce new 'Granges.' In order to avoid duplication, Bachmann opts to produce a 'Hall' and Hornby's model hits the shelves this year.

2015   Dapol releases first 'N' gauge 'Grange'.

ABOVE: **Hornby 'OO' gauge 'Grange' is not in the 2025 catalogue.**

ABOVE: **Dapol's 'N' gauge 'Grange' is not in the 2025 catalogue.**

Detail differences

Original condition

A: Narrow 'Grange'-type chimney. 6800-6803 originally built with cast iron chimneys
B: Oil pipe covers (on fireman's side)

ABOVE: Rail Archive Stephenson/Rail Online

Final condition

A: Some engines fitted with 'Improved Draughting' chimneys, similar to the 'Hall's', circa 1960 onwards.
B: Fireman's side oil pipe covers removed. This is a subject not covered in the wealth of books and it seems to coincide with fitting 'ID' chimneys. Evidence suggests that additional cover on driver's side of boiler, close to firebox, was added at the same time.

ABOVE: R. Green/Colour Rail

SUBSCRIBE TODAY!

WHICH *HORNBY MAGAZINE* SUBSCRIPTION SUITS YOU BEST?

A 12 MONTH SUBSCRIPTION

BEST VALUE

UK PRINT - 1 year

£59.99*

Paying by Annual Direct Debit

PLUS A FREE GIFT!
Choose from Gift A or B

B 6 MONTH SUBSCRIPTION

UK PRINT - 6 months

£31.00

Paying by 6-Month Direct Debit

PLUS A FREE GIFT!
Gift B ONLY

FREE GIFT
Choose <u>one</u> of the following...

Gift A
Or
Gift B

WORTH £34.00!

WORTH £17.99!

Gift A, Great Electric Train Show tickets, only available on UK 12-month subscriptions.

REASONS TO SUBSCRIBE TO *HORNBY MAGAZINE*..

》 **EXCLUSIVE** Subscriber offers across books, specials, limited editions and modelling essentials 》 **SAVE** - *Hornby Magazine* subscribers can **SAVE £20** on Railway Touring Company main line steam trip tickets! 》 **NEVER MISS AN ISSUE** - delivered direct to your door every month 》 **DISCOUNTS** on The Great Electric Train Show and Model World LIVE event tickets 》 **BE THE FIRST** to read the latest features 》 **FREE GIFT** for new UK print 1 year subscriptions

SCAN HERE TO SUBSCRIBE TODAY!

The 'Manor' 4-6-0

The 'Manors' became synonymous with one particular named Western Region train: the 'Cambrian Coast Express'. They might not have been the most successful of all the GWR 4-6-0s but the 'Manors' are very pretty locomotives, as 7810 *Draycott Manor* illustrates at Dovey Junction on July 24 1963. It's waiting for a Standard '4MT' 2-6-4T to arrive with the Pwllheli portion of the 'CCE', which will be added to the train it has brought from Aberystwyth. Brian Stephenson/Rail Online

Designer	Charles Collett
Lifespan	1938-1965
GWR power class	D (BR '5MT')
GWR route restriction	Blue

Charles Collett couldn't have been more different to George Jackson Churchward. Churchward not only had a genius bent but behaved like a down-to-earth, rough-hewn country squire, his approachable attitude generating loyalty from those around him.

Collett was a good engineer and he rose through the ranks to become Churchward's right hand man. He was urbane yet aloof and didn't mix well with his workforce. The death of his beloved wife Ethelwyn in March 1923, just over a year after being appointed Churchward's successor in January 1922, profoundly affected him as he shifted his focus from locomotive design to spiritualism and studying the paranormal.

Generally speaking, he was loathe to deviate from Churchward's general principles, other than, say, minor tweaks to wheel diameters. This stemmed from an incident with the pioneer '56XX' 0-6-2T, a radical departure from anything Churchward had designed, which failed on its first steaming and required a hurried re-design of key motion parts. The next time Collett and his team came unstuck was when designing the 'Manors'.

While Collett had designed bigger boilers than Churchward had, they maintained the same successful proportions. But the 'Manors' required a smaller boiler than usual.

The 'Grange' (see p78) was built to replace the '43XX' 2-6-0s, which had been introduced in 1911. They were perfect mixed traffic on Blue routes, in line with route 17t 12cwt axle weight restrictions. But the 'Grange' was a Red route engine (20t axle loading) and couldn't take over duties from '43XXs' on Blue routes.

Collett's solution for reducing weight in the 'Grange' was to fit it with a smaller boiler. Rather than, say, re-use the '43XX's' No. 4 boiler, Collett and his team designed the new No. 14. It was over 2ft shorter than the 'Grange's' No. 1 and about 3in narrower in diameter. Both the grate and the superheater surface area were smaller too.

GWR fireman Harold Gasson recalled, "The 'Grange' could be worked hard with always a little bit in reserve but not the 'Manor'. They appeared so sluggish. They had no poke."

It was a view shared by Kenneth Leech. "My only clear memory of the 'Manors' is of the disappointment I felt on my first trip on one, both as regards steaming and power."

Yet, the 'Manor' has become something of a cult classic with Western aficionados and that's because of a wartime relaxation over what could work the former Cambrian Railways' network. It was a relaxation that became permanent and the 'Manors' became 'Top Link' power on the Cambrian, until the line was transferred to the London Midland Region in the mid-1960s.

Images of 'Manors' powering through the stunning North Wales scenery, hauling the famous 'Cambrian Coast Express' with the white smokebox embellishments of Aberystwyth shedmaster Danny Rowlands, have cemented the class as a Western favourite. Their reputation was certainly repaired once experiments at Swindon in 1951/52 fixed their draughting.

The 'Manors' are now the second most represented GWR 4-6-0 in preservation. That's because 11 were still in service in the final months of 1965, the final year of Western Region steam. Of those 11, nine were based at Shrewsbury while 7808 *Cookham Manor* and 7829 *Ramsbury Manor* were at Gloucester Horton Road. Woodham Brothers swooped in to buy those at Shrewsbury while the Great Western Society bought *Cookham Manor*; only last-built 7829 slipped through the net.

MANOR - KEY DIMENSIONS				
Dimensions	Prototype	1:76 scale	1:148 scale	1:43 scale
Length (over buffers)	61ft 9¼in	247.6mm	127.4mm	433.7mm
Height (over cab)	13ft 0in	52mm	26.7mm	91mm
Width (over cylinders)	8ft 10⅞in	32.4mm	16.6mm	56.7mm
Wheel diameter (driving)	5ft 8in	23.2mm	11.9mm	40.6mm
Wheel diameter (bogie)	3ft 0in	12mm	6.1mm	21mm
Wheel diameter (tender)	4ft 1½in	16.4mm	8.4mm	28.7mm
Cylinders (2)	18in by 30in	-	-	-

NUMBERS AND BUILDS			
Engine Nos.	Lot No.	Building dates	Works/ Builder
7800-7819	316	1938-39	Swindon
7820-7829	377	1950	Swindon
Total: 30			

ABOVE: Colour Rail

WHERE WERE THEY SHEDDED?		
Shed name	GWR code	BR code
Banbury	BAN	84C
Bristol Bath Road	BRD	82A
Bristol St Philips Marsh	SPM	82B
Cardiff Canton*	CDF	86C
Cardiff East Dock	CED	88B
Carmarthen	CARM	87G
Cheltenham Malvern Road	CHEL	85B
Chester West	CHR	84K
Croes Newydd	CNYD	84J
		89B (1960-1963)
		6C (1963-1967)
Didcot	DID	81E
Gloucester Horton Road	GLO	83D
Hereford	SRD	84A
Leamington	LMTN	84D
Llanelli	LLY	87F
Machynlleth	MCH	89C
		6F (1963-1966)
Neath Court Sart	NEA	87A
Newton Abbot	NA	83A

(CONT'D)		
Shed name	GWR code	BR code
Neyland	NEY	87H
Newton Abbot	NA	83A
Oswestry	OSY	89A
		89D
Penzance	PZ	83G
		84D
Plymouth Laira	LA	83D
Reading	RDG	81D
Severn Tunnel Junction	STJ	86E
		6F (1963-1966)
Shrewsbury	SALOP	84G
St Blazey	SBZ	83E
		84C
Stourbridge Junction	STB	84F
Swansea Landore	LDR	
Swindon	SDN	
Taunton	TB	83B
Truro	TR	83F
Tyseley	TYS	84E
Wolverhampton Oxley	OXY	84B
Worcester	WOS	85A

'Manor' liveries

1938-1940

1940-1947

1948-1956

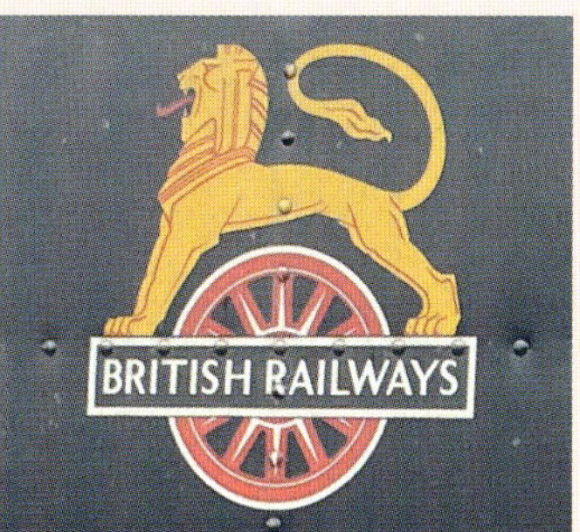

Circa 1956

1956-1966

CAN I SEE ONE?

The final two 'Manors' were withdrawn in December 1965. Nine survive: 7802 *Bradley Manor* (Severn Valley Railway), 7808 *Cookham Manor* (Didcot Railway Centre), 7812 *Erlestoke Manor* (SVR), 7819 *Hinton Manor* (SVR), 7820 *Dinmore Manor* (Gloucestershire Warwickshire Steam Railway), 7821 *Ditcheat Manor* (Swindon Designer Outlet) 7822 *Foxcote Manor* (Tyseley Locomotive Works), 7827 *Lydham Manor* (Dartmouth Steam Railway), and 7828 *Odney Manor* (West Somerset Railway).

'Manor' tenders

Churchward 3,500gal (long fender)

Model timeline

1985   Remaining stocks of Mainline's 'Manor', new in 1980, are released under the Dapol brand. Dapol had bought the 'OO' gauge Mainline range of model railways from Palitoy, after it was closed by its parent company General Mills.

1991   The old Mainline 'Manor' reappears under the Bachmann Branchline brand.

2008   Anglo-Australian firm Ixion announces a new 'N' gauge 'Manor'. When it arrives the following year, it's found to be 8% under scale.

2010   Ixion's re-tooled 'N' gauge 'Manor' hits the shelves. This is the last year that the Branchline 'OO' gauge 'Manor' is available new.

2011   Ixion's 'N' gauge 'Manor' is sold to Dapol

2020   Dapol announces that it is working on an all-new 'OO' gauge 'Manor'. This goes on sale in 2022.

2021   Accurascale announces its first 'OO' gauge steam model – and it's a 'Manor'. It goes on sale in 2023.

2024   Dapol announces that it is to develop an all-new 'N' gauge 'Manor'.

Dapol 'OO' gauge 'Manor'

- 4S-001-008   7820 *Dinmore Manor*, BR lined black
- 4S-001-009   7818 *Granville Manor*, GWR roundel
- 4S-001-010   7806 *Cockington Manor*, GWR green
- 4S-001-011   7821 *Ditcheat Manor*, BR lined black
- 4S-001-012   7822 *Foxcote Manor*, BR black
- 4S-001-013   7817 *Garsington Manor*, BR green
- 4S-001-014   7802 *Bradley Manor*, BR lined green

RRP: From £165.55.
Availability: Dapol stockists
or *www.dapol.com*

Dapol 'N' gauge 'Manor'

- 2S-001-005   7818 *Granville Manor*, GWR roundel
- 2S-001-006   7814 *Fringford Manor*, GWR initials
- 2S-001-007   7807 *Compton Manor*, G crest W livery
- 2S-001-008   7800 *Torquay Manor*, BR lined black early
- 2S-001-009   7810 *Draycott Manor*, BR lined green early
- 2S-001-010   7803 *Barcote Manor*, BR lined green late
- 2S-001-011   7808 *Cookham Manor*, BR lined green late

RRP: From £190.00. Availability: Dapol stockists or *www.dapol.com*

STOP PRESS: Although currently sold out, Accurascale has announced a second run of five 'Manors' due to be released in late 2026.

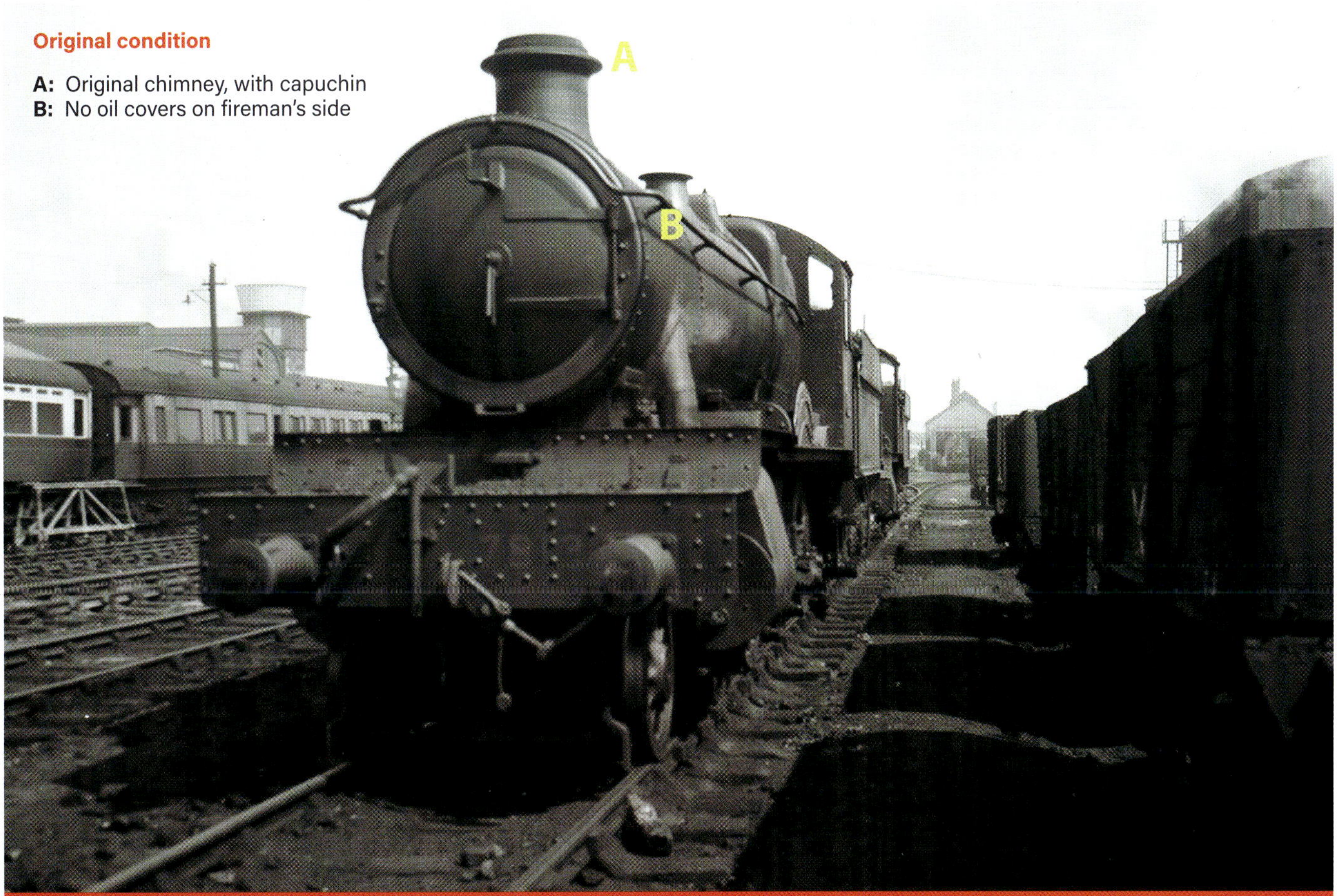
Original condition
A: Original chimney, with capuchin
B: No oil covers on fireman's side
A
B

ABOVE: John Hilmer/Colour Rail

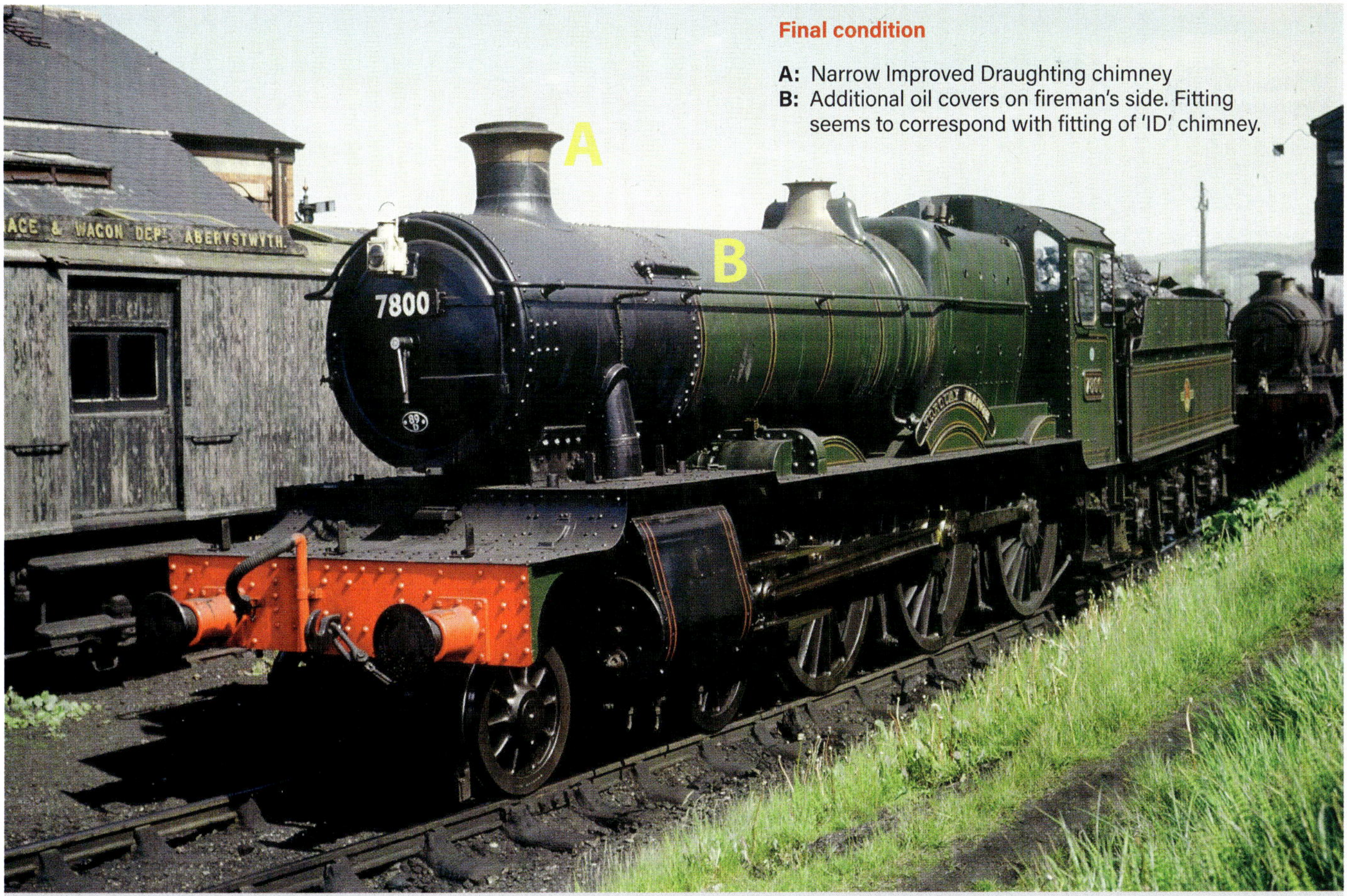
Final condition
A: Narrow Improved Draughting chimney
B: Additional oil covers on fireman's side. Fitting seems to correspond with fitting of 'ID' chimney.
A
B
7800

ABOVE: Colour Rail

The 'Modified Hall' 4-6-0

Designer	F.W. Hawksworth
Lifespan	1944-1966
GWR power class	D (BR '5MT')
GWR route restriction	Red

Charles Collett retired in 1941 and was replaced by Frederick William Hawksworth. He was a Swindon man through and through, having joined the GWR as an apprentice in 1898. He moved up the ranks at Swindon, from apprentice draughtsman in 1905 to Principal Assistant, effectively acting as Collett's right-hand man.

Most new Chief Mechanical Engineers make their mark with a raft of new designs but Hawksworth was appointed at an inopportune time. Wartime restrictions meant that Swindon was only able to build things like 'Halls', '2884' 2-8-0s and pannier tanks; essentially, engines for hauling and shunting vital goods trains. If Hawksworth had any ideas for new express engines, it would have to wait.

However, wartime conditions were causing different issues. GWR motive power that worked beautifully before the war was now struggling with poor quality coal and a lack of maintenance. Hawksworth set out to make some improvements to the 'Hall', to make it more suitable for wartime – and post-war – conditions.

The already excellent No. 1 boiler was made even better by fitting a three-row superheater. The Churchward frame arrangement, with a front subframe/cylinder block assembly was replaced by plate frames throughout and a fabricated smokebox saddle. And the Swindon/de Glehn bogie was replaced by a simple plate frame bogie with a 2ft longer wheelbase.

The first of the new class slipped in behind the last of the original 'Halls'. As that first engine was numbered 6959, the class was designated '6959'. But they have long been known as 'Modified Halls'. Being a wartime build, the first batch of 'Modified Halls' entered service with neither names nor cabside windows.

BELOW: 'Modified Hall' 6999 *Capel Dewi Hall* looks impatient for the off at Cardiff General on July 9 1956 with the Down 'Red Dragon'. This is a photograph that highlights that all the 'Hall' family were capable of hauling the very heaviest trains. R.O. Tuck/Rail Archive Stephenson/Rail Online

Construction continued after the war, the locomotives emerging from Swindon with nameplates. Having designed a handsome, new straight-sided tender for his 'Counties' (see page 40), a version was designed for the 'Modified Halls'.

No. 6990 *Witherslack Hall*, finished in full Great Western Railway livery, represented the Western Region during the 1948 Exchange Trials, where the newly formed British Railways pitted the designs from the former 'Big Four' against each other, the result of which would influence the design of its new Standard steam locomotives. Construction of the 'Modified Halls continued until 1950, a year after Hawksworth resigned. He might have only had five new designs accredited to him but 'his' locomotives – the '94XX' 0-6-0PTs – were still being delivered in 1956, just four years before BR stopped building new steam locomotives.

The 'Modified Hall', for all of their minor changes from the rules that Churchward laid down nearly half a century before, were still highly capable machines. Tyseley engineman Dick Potts recalled that the last of the class, 7929 *Wyke Hall*, was the best of the lot. It was so free-steaming that it reportedly did a 350-mile trip with 12 coaches on just one tender of coal.

MODIFIED HALL' - KEY DIMENSIONS

Table of dimensions	Prototype	1:76 scale	1:148 scale	1:43 scale
Length (over buffers)	63ft ¼in	252.6mm	129.7mm	441.4mm
Height (over cab)	13ft 2¹⁄₁₆in	52.9mm	27.1mm	92.4mm
Width (over cylinders)	8ft 11¼in	36mm	18.5mm	63mm
Wheel diameter (driving)	6ft 0in	24mm	12.3mm	42mm
Wheel diameter (bogie)	3ft 0in	12mm	6.1mm	21mm
Wheel diameter (tender)	4ft 1½in	16.4mm	8.4mm	28.7mm
Cylinders (2)	18½in by 30in	-	-	-

ABOVE: Rail Photoprints

NUMBERS AND BUILDS

Engine Nos.	Lot No.	Building dates	Works/Builder
6959-6970	350	March 1944-September 1944	Swindon
6971-6990	366	October 1947-April 1948	Swindon
6991-7919	368	November 1948-May 1950	Swindon
7920-7929	376	September 1950-November 1950	Swindon

WHERE WERE THEY SHEDDED?

Shed name	GWR code	BR code
Banbury	BAN	84C
Bristol Bath Road	BRD	82A
Bristol St Philips Marsh	SPM	82B
Bristol Barrow Road		82E*
Cardiff Canton*	CDF	86C
Cardiff East Dock	CED	88B
Carmarthen	CARM	87G
Chester West	CHR	84K
Didcot	DID	81E
Duffryn Yard	DYD	87B
Ebbw Junction	NA	83A
Exeter	EXE	83A
Fishguard Goodwick	FDG	81A
Gloucester Horton Road	GLO	83D
Hereford	SRD	84A
Neath Court Sart	NEA	87A
Newton Abbot	NA	83A
Neyland	NEY	87H
Old Oak Common	PDN	81A

(CONT'D)

Shed name	GWR code	BR code
Oxford	OXF	81F
Plymouth Laira	LA	83D
Reading	RDG	81D
Salisbury	WES	82D
Severn Tunnel Junction	STJ	86E
Shrewsbury	SALOP	84G
Southall	SHL	81C
St Blazey	SBZ	83E
Stourbridge Junction	STB	84F
Swindon	SDN	82C
Swansea Landore	LDR	87E
Taunton	TB	83B
Tyseley	TYS	84E
Westbury	WES	82D
Weymouth Radipole	WEY	82F
Wolverhampton Oxley	OXY	84B
Wolverhampton Stafford Road	SRD	84A
Worcester	WOS	85A
* London Midland Region shed until 1958		

'Modified Hall' liveries

1944-1945*

1945-48

1948-1956

Circa 1956

1956-1966

RIGHT: Trevor Owen/Colour Rail

Tenders

Collett 4,000gal (Nos. 6959-6970 new)

Hawksworth 4,000gal (Nos. 6971-7929 new)

CAN I SEE ONE?

6998 *Burton Agnes Hall* was officially withdrawn on December 31 1965 but hauled the 2.10pm Bournemouth-York from Oxford to Banbury on January 3 1966, the last steam-hauled service on the Western Region (Somerset & Dorset excepted). Six survive: 6960 *Raveningham Hall* (One:One Collection), 6984 *Owsden Hall* and 6989 *Wightwick Hall* (Buckinghamshire Railway Centre), 6990 *Witherslack Hall* (Great Central Railway), 6998 *Burton Agnes Hall* (Didcot Railway Centre) and 7903 *Foremarke Hall* (Gloucestershire Warwickshire Steam Railway).

Model timeline

1990   Replica Railways finally fulfils Mainline's 1984 plan to produce a 'OO' gauge 'Modified Hall'. The new model uses Mainline's design work with a few improvements.

1996   The Replica model now appears under the new Bachmann Branchline brand.

2013   Bachmann Branchline uses its 2005 'Hall' tooling (p71) to produce an all new, 21st century standard 'Modified Hall'. However, it features myriad errors and is recalled, with only a few models making it onto the market.

2015   Bachmann makes another attempt at producing the 'Modified Hall'. Many of the previous errors are fixed but the front frame arrangement is wrong.

2021   Third attempt at the 'Modified Hall' appears, with all errors fixed. It's not in the 2025 Bachmann Branchline range but models are still available new.

Third time lucky: Bachmann Branchline's third attempt at the 'Modified Hall', not in the 2025 range.

Detail differences

Almost as built

A: Cab windows plated over (6959-6970)
B: Cast iron chimney with capuchin
C: Sight-feed lubricator

RIGHT: John Hilmer/Colour Rail

Mid condition

A: Speedometer (introduced from 1960 to selected engines)
B: Additional cover introduced 1950s
C: Two-row superheater

RIGHT: Colour Rail

Final condition

A: Three-row superheater
B: Narrow 'improved draughting' chimney
C: Mechanical lubricator (introduced from 7910 and fitted to earlier engines)
D: Extra cover, presumably (the books are quiet on this) connected to the new superheaters.

BELOW: Trevor Owen/ Colour Rail

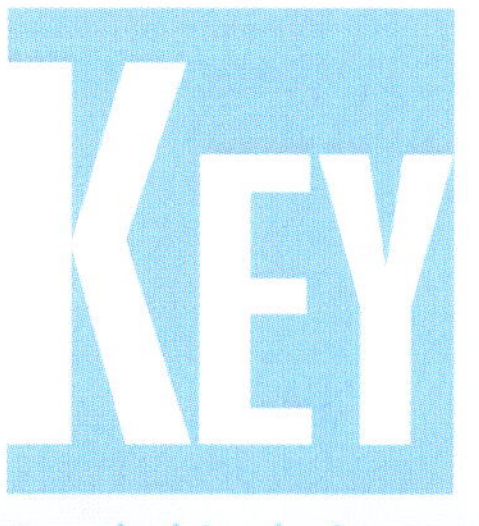

THE DESTINATION FOR RAIL MODELLING ENTHUSIASTS

Visit us today and discover all our latest releases

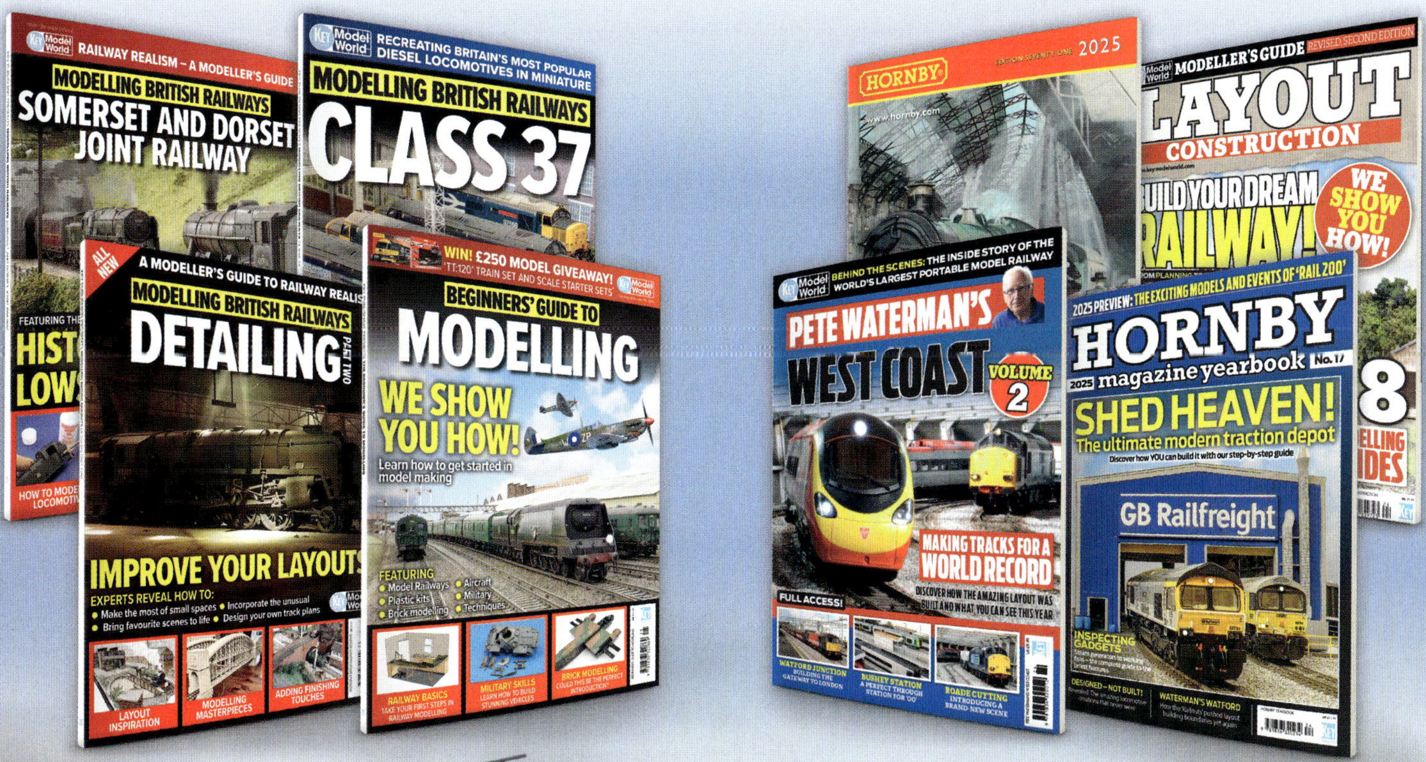

Order from our online shop today...

shop.keymodelworld.com/specials

Call +44 (0)1780 480404 *(Monday to Friday 9am - 5.30pm GMT)*

**Free 2nd class P&P on BFPO orders. Overseas charges apply.*

'Modified Hall' 7903 *Foremarke Hall*, new 'Grange' 6880 *Betton Grange*, new 'Saint' 2999 *Lady of Legend* and 'Manor' 7820 *Dinmore Manor* prepare for the day ahead at the Gloucestershire Warwickshire Steam Railway's Toddington shed on May 24 2024. Paul Chancellor

Inspirational days out

Want to see surviving GWR express engines? Here are some locations to go for a top notch GWR-themed day out

ABOVE: Pioneer 'Castle' 4073 *Caerphilly Castle* is one of the highlights of a visit to STEAM-The Museum of the GWR at Swindon. The 1923 4-6-0 was displayed at the Science Museum in London from 1961 until the late 1990s, when it moved to the enlarged museum in Swindon. Paul Chancellor

You can study all the books in the world but there's nothing like seeing the thing you want to model first-hand. Happily, there are plenty of places to go to see the cream of GWR express passenger power... often at work.

Didcot Railway Centre has to be top of the list. It's the headquarters of the Great Western Society, formed in the 1960s when four schoolboys decided to save a humble '14XX' 0-4-2T and Autocoach. Since then, the GWS collection has grown to include examples of almost every class included in this publication: one 'King', two 'Castles', two 'Halls' (Collett and Hawksworth) and one 'Manor'. It's also leading the way in filling the missing gaps, having successfully built a new 'Saint' while a new Hawksworth 'County' is nearing completion. And, it's also home to gas turbine 18000.

What makes Didcot such an inspirational day out is that this collection is housed in the original GWR steam shed, dating from 1932. It's also a great place to see GWR coaches... in fact, it's perfect for immersing yourself in all things GWR.

Just under 40 miles west from Didcot is STEAM-The Museum of the GWR at Swindon. Housed in part of the former Swindon Works site, the museum is home to key GWR express passenger power, such as the last surviving 'City' and 'Star' (3717 *City of Truro* and 4003 *Lode Star*) as well as the first 'Castle' (4073 *Caerphilly Castle*) and 'King' (6000 *King George V*). Be aware, though, that, as part of the National Collection, 3717, 4003 and 6000 do split their time between Swindon and the National Railway Museum at York so it's worth contacting before making a visit to avoid disappointment.

Although you can't visit Vintage Trains' Tyseley base or Locomotive Services' Crewe headquarters (except on special open days), you can experience their locomotives out on the main line. Vintage Trains operates two 'Castles' (5043 *Earl of Mount Edgcumbe* and 7029 *Clun Castle*) while LSL's 5029 *Nunney Castle* is set to be joined by 'King' 6024 *King Edward I* in the hopefully not too distant future.

There are plenty of preserved railways where you can experience GWR 4-6-0s in action: the Severn Valley Railway is home to 'Halls' and 'Manors', as is the West Somerset Railway while the Gloucestershire Warwickshire Steam Railway can offer both classes as well as being the nominal home for new build 'Grange' 6880 *Betton Grange*.

ABOVE: 'Castle' 4079 *Pendennis Castle* is one of the jewels in the Great Western Society's collection, which also includes classmate 5051 *Drysllwyn Castle* and 'King' 6023 *King Edward II* as well as a new 'Saint' and 'County', all housed in the genuine GWR steam shed at Didcot. Both: Richard Foster

Modelling the trains

Model locomotives need trains to pull. Here's how to model classic named trains from the GWR/Western Region.

t's a sad fact that the choice of ready-to-run Great Western Railway coaches does not reflect the range of available locomotives... at least coaches for the 'Top Link' duties that we're talking about here.

In 'OO' gauge, Hornby has produced four types of Hawksworth 64ft coaches (introduced 1947, the models in 2010) and four types of Collett 'Bow Ended' stock (introduced 1925, the models in 2016). Bachmann periodically offers the Collett Diagram E159 and C77 'Excursion Stock' models that date back to Mainline days while the old Airfix 'Centenary' stock hasn't been produced by Hornby for some years.

'N' gauge modellers have even less choice: three diagrams of Collett 'Excursion' stock from Dapol and two types of Hawksworth 64ft stock from Graham Farish.

That makes it rather tricky to put together accurate train formations for the GWR era.

The GWR only ran five named services up to the Second World War. The oldest and arguably most famous was the 'Cornish Riviera'. This was launched in July 1904 but wasn't named until circa 1906. Its name would switch between the 'Limited' and 'Express' suffix so it's worth checking photographic evidence to reflect the period you're modelling.

Trains such as the 'Riviera' evolved over time, the timings adjusted, stops amended or altered. Therefore, a typical summer 'Cornish Riviera' would leave Paddington at 10.10am bound for Penzance, running non-stop to Plymouth. This train would contain coaches for St. Ives, Falmouth, Newquay and Kingsbridge, that, once detached, would be hauled to their destinations behind branch passenger workings. It would also, depending on the time of year, include coaches for Weymouth and Ilfracombe which would be slipped – uncoupled without stopping and brought to a stand by the guard – at Westbury and Taunton. The Up train would depart Penzance at 10am, collecting coaches from the coastal resorts, bound for London.

As the GWR's premier train, the 'Riveria' periodically received new stock. New coaches – 60ft long and 9ft 5¾in wide – comprising 13 different diagrams were introduced in 1929. These were superseded

'King' 6028 *King George VI* approaches Twyford, to the east of Reading, with the 'Bristolian' on May 27 1959. Six of the seven coaches are BR Mk Is, with a GWR 12w dining car just to the left of the signal. Trevor Owen/Colour Rail

in 1935 when the first of the 'Centenary' coaches were introduced. Although 60ft long, they were 9ft 7in wide and were designed to mark 100 years since the Great Western Railway Act 1835 was passed by Parliament.

Torbay Express

It's not clear when the 'Torbay Express' gained its name but it was in existence

RIGHT: 'King' 6008 *King James II* approaches Wellington, Somerset, with the 10.30am Down 'Cornish Riviera Express' in 1928. The train comprises a mixture of stock; this is seven years before the 'Centenary' stock is introduced on this, arguably the GWR's most famous named train.
F.R. Hebron/Rail Archive Stephenson/Rail Online

TRAIN FORMATIONS

Departure time	Name	Route	Era	Formation	
8.45am	Bristolian	London-Bristol	1957/58 Winter Timetable	Mk I SK(MO)	Mk I BCK
10am	Bristolian	London-Bristol	1936	D121	C70
9am	Inter-City	London-Wolverhampton	1957/58 Winter Timetable	Mk I BSK	Mk I SK
9am	Cornishman	Wolverhampton-Penzance	1961 Summer Timetable	Penzance:	Mk I BSK
				Kingswear:	Mk I SK
9.55am	South Wales Pullman	London-Swansea	Aug-60	PKT No. 54	PKT No. 171
10.10am	Cambrian Coast Express	London-Aberystwyth/Pwllheli	1957/58 Winter Timetable	Pwllheli:	Mk I BSK
				Aberystwyth:	GWR RC
N/a	N/a	Fishguard-London	June, 1935	H17/18	H15
10.30am	Cornish Riviera Express	London-Plymouth-Penzance	1961 Summer Timetable	Penzance:	Mk I BSK
				Plymouth:	Mk I SK
10am	Cornish Riviera Limited	Plymouth-London	Mid-1930s	C59	C70
10.55am	Pembroke Coast Express	London-Swansea-Pembroke Dock	1961 Summer Timetable	Pembroke:	Mk I BSK
				Swansea:	Mk I SK
11.15am	Merchant Venturer	London-Weston-super-Mare	1957/58 Winter Timetable	Mk I BSK	Mk I SK
12pm	Torbay Express	London-Kingswear	1957/58 Winter Timetable	Mk I BSK	Mk I SK
N/a	Plymouth-London	Ocean Mail	Mid-1930s	M10	H46
1.30pm	Royal Duchy	London-Penzance	1957/58 Winter Timetable	Penzance:	Mk I BSK
				Kingswear:	Mk I CK
3.55pm	Capitals United Express	London-Neyland-Fishguard Harbour	1961 Summer Timetable	Neyland:	Mk I BSK
				Fishguard Harbour:	
				Swansea:	Mk I BSK
				Swansea-Carmarthen:	
4.45pm	Cathedrals Express	London-Hereford	1957/58 Winter Timetable	Hereford:	Mk I BSK
				Kidderminster	Mk I FK
				Worcester:	GWR CK (FO)
5pm	Cheltenham Spa Express	London-Cheltenham	1961 Summer Timetable	Mk I BSK	Mk I SK
5.30pm	Mayflower	London-Plymouth	1957/58 Winter Timetable	Plymouth:	Mk I BSK
				Kingswear:	Mk I BSK (FO)
5.55pm	Red Dragon	London-Cardiff-Carmarthen	1957/58 Winter Timetable	Cardiff:	Mk I BCK
				Swansea:	Mk I BCK
				Carmarthen:	Mk I BSK

MO=Mondays Only
FO=Fridays Only

before the First World War. By the start of the Second World War, it would leave London at 12pm, arriving at Exeter St Davids at 2.49pm, Torquay 35 minutes later, and terminating at Kingswear, on the River Dart estuary, at 4.55pm. The Up train, having already tackled severe gradients on the single-line from Kingswear, would depart Torquay at 12pm and arrive into Paddington at 3.35pm.

As a footnote to the story, the 'Torquay Express' was complemented by the 'Torquay Pullman Limited', which was launched on July 8 1929. It left London at 11am, arriving into Paignton at 2.50pm, the same train returning to London at 4.50pm and arriving at 8.30pm. The train comprised eight Pullman cars but the GWR found the cost of hiring staff and vehicles prohibitive and the service ceased in 1931. Also ending that year was the use of Pullman coaches in 'Boat' trains to the coastal ports. Instead, the GWR chose to build eight 'Super Saloons', designed to rival the luxury of a Pullman Car.

The opening of a joint line with the Great Central Railway between Northolt, northwest London and Ashendon Junction, halfway between Princes Risborough and Bicester, in 1910, enabled the GWR to complete for traffic between London, Birmingham/Wolverhampton and Birkenhead on Merseyside. But connections at Shrewsbury also meant access to the Welsh coastal resorts, particularly Aberystwyth.

An express from Paddington with portions for Aberystwyth and Pwllheli was launched in 1921, the operation becoming easier after the 1923 Grouping, and the Cambrian Railways main line becoming part of the GWR network. It was named the 'Cambrian Coast Express' in 1927.

Until 1939, it departed Paddington at 10.10am. At Wolverhampton, the 'Castle' or 'King' was swapped for a 4-4-0 – usually a 'Duke' (or two) but later a 'Manor' – for the run west, calling at Welshpool, Machynlleth, Dovey Junction and Borth, arriving into Aberystwyth at 3.55pm. The Up train would leave Aberystwyth at 10am, due in at Paddington at 4pm.

The story of the 'Cheltenham Spa Express' began when an additional afternoon service between Cheltenham, Gloucester and Paddington was added to the timetable just after the First World War.

Mk I SK	Mk I SK	Dia. H55 RB	Mk I FK	Mk I FK	Mk I BCK				
E151	H41	E151	C70	D121					
Mk I SK	Mk I SK	GWR RC	Mk I FK	Mk I FK	Mk I FK	Mk I BCK			
Mk I SK	Mk I SK	Mk I CK	Mk I RU	MK I SO	Mk I SK	Mk I BSK			
Mk I CK	Mk I SK	Mk I BSK	Mk I SK (FO)						
PSP No. 35	Daffodil Bar	PFK Cecilia	PFP Zena	PFK Chloria	PKT No. 27				
Mk I SK	Mk I CK	Mk I CK							
Mk I FK	Mk I SK	Mk I BSK							
E137	D43	E79/81	D111	D43	E109	M14			
Mk I SK	Mk I SK	Mk I SK	Dia H40 RSO	Dia H39 RF	Mk I FK	Mk I CK	Mk I BSK		
Mk I BCK									
E150	E150	D120	E149	H47	H48	C69x2	D120	E150	E148
Mk I SK	Mk I FK	Mk I BSK							
Mk I RU	Mk I FO	Mk I CK	Mk I BSK						
Mk I SK	Mk I FK	Mk I FK	GWR RC	Mk I SK	Mk I SK	Mk I BSK			
Mk I SK	Mk I SK	GWR RC	Mk I FK	Mk I FK	Mk I BSK				
G60	H45	H40	H39	E109/11	C44	D82/84			
Mk I SK	Mk I SK	Mk I SK	GWR RC	Mk I FK	Mk I BSK				
Mk I SK	Mk I BSK								
Mk I CK									
Mk I FK	Mk I SK	Mk I BSK							
Mk I FK	Mk I RU	Mk I SO	Mk I SK	Mk I BSK					
GWR SK(FO)	GWR SK								
Mk I SK	Mk I SK	GWR RC	Mk I FK	Mk I BSK					
Mk I FK	Mk I SK	Mk I BSK							
Mk I SK	Mk I CK	Mk I SO	Mk I RU	Mk I FK	Mk I FK	Mk I BCK	Mk I SK (FO)		
Mk I SK (MFO)	Mk I SK	GWR RSO	GWR RF	Mk I FK	Mk I BSK				
Mk I SK (FO)	Mk I FK	Mk I SK	Mk I BSK	Mk I SK (FO)					
Mk I SK	Mk I FK	GWR RF	GWR RSO						
Mk I CK									
Mk I FK	Mk I SK	Mk I SK	Mk I SK	Mk I BSK					

		BUYING THE COACHES			
Code	**Builder**	**Description**	**OO gauge**	**N gauge**	**O gauge**
Mk I FK	BR Mk I	Corridor First	Branchline/Hornby	Graham Farish	Lionheart
Mk I SK	BR Mk I	Corridor Second	Branchline/Hornby	Graham Farish	Lionheart
Mk I CK	BR Mk I	Corridor Composite	Branchline/Hornby	Graham Farish	Lionheart
MK I SO	BR Mk I	Second Open	Branchline/Hornby	Graham Farish	Lionheart
Mk I BCK	BR Mk I	Brake Corridor Composite	Branchline/Hornby	Graham Farish	Lionheart
Mk I BSK	BR Mk I	Brake Corridor Second	Branchline/Hornby	Graham Farish	Lionheart
Mk I RU	BR Mk I	Restaurant Unclassified	Branchline	Graham Farish	Darstaed
PFP	Pullman Car	Pullman Parlour First	Hornby	Revolution	Darstaed
PKT	Pullman Car	Pullman Kitchen Third	Hornby	Revolution	Darstaed
PSP	Pullman Car	Pullman Parlour Second	Hornby	-	Darstaed
PFK	Pullman Car	Pullman Kitchen First	Hornby	Revolution	Darstaed
PKP	Pullman Car	Pullman Parlour First	Hornby	Revolution	Darstaed
Daffodil Bar	Pullman Car	Daffodil Bar	Hornby	-	-
Dia. H55 RB	GWR	Diagram H55 12w Buffet	Phoenix	-	-
Dia H40 RTO	GWR	Diagram H40 Restaurant Third Open	Comet	-	-
Dia H39 RF	GWR	Diagram H39 Restaurant First	Comet	-	-
GWR RC	GWR	Diagram H25 57ft Restaurant Composite	Comet	-	-
	GWR	Diagram H57 61ft Restaurant Composite	Comet	-	-
GWR SK(FO)	GWR	Corridor Second	-	-	-
GWR CK (FO)		Corridor Composite	Hornby Hawksworth or Branchline Collett	Graham Farish Hawksworth	-

The stretch of the East Coast Main Line between Darlington and York was level and ideally suited for high speed running, which it had proved as home to Britain's fastest train: 44.1 miles in 43 minutes.

But Brunel had engineered the GWR main line between Swindon and London as a high speed railway too and so the GWR started to accelerate this afternoon express in 1923.

Although the famous square headboard would later say 'Cheltenham Flyer', it was always officially called the 'Cheltenham Spa Express'. In 1929, the 'Flyer' was timed to run the 77.3 miles from Swindon and Paddington in just 70 minutes The average speed was 66.2mph. Already exceeding the LNERs timings, a threat from Canada forced the GWR to accelerate the timings further in September 1932: 65 minutes and an average speed of 71.4mph.

The high point of the 'Flyer's' career came on June 6 1932 when 'Castle' 5006 *Tregenna Castle* ran the 77.3 miles in 56min 47 seconds, an average speed of 81.7mph!

Sadly, the 'Flyer' didn't remain the world's fastest train for long. It was soon bettered by the LNER's 'Coronation' to name but one but retained its 71.4mph average speed until the start of the war.

The Bristolian

The last of the named quintet was the 'Bristolian', introduced in 1935 to mark the GWR's centenary. It ran non-stop between London and Bristol and was timed for 105 minutes in both directions. Down trains used the full length of Brunel's original main line into Bristol Temple Meads. However, Up trains headed north to Filton Junction and then ran east on the Badminton Cut-off, to reach the original main line at Wootton Bassett.

The 'Bristolian' departed Paddington at 10am, the Up train leaving Temple Meads at 4.30pm. In his seminal book *Titled Trains of Great Britain*, Cecil J. Allen says that the train used coaches of the "latest wide types, with recessed end doors." The final coaches that the GWR built to this design were the

ABOVE: **'Castle' 5031 *Totnes Castle* speeds through Wilmcote, to the north of Stratford-upon-Avon, with the 'Cornishman' in June 1954. The leading coach is of GWR origin. This was the one of the few Western Region named trains that didn't originate/terminate at London Paddington, running from the Midlands instead.** Rail Photoprints

ABOVE: **'Castle' 5080 *Defiant* passes Rumney Bridge, near Cardiff, with the Up 'South Wales Pullman' on June 6 1957. This was one of the few Pullman services to run on the GWR/Western Region; it would later be replaced with one of the 'Blue Pullman' diesel units.** R.O. Tuck/Rail Archive Stephenson/Rail Online

ABOVE: **'Manor' 7828 *Odney Manor* blasts up Talerddig, the fearsome climb between Machynlleth and Newtown, with the Up 'Cambrian Coast Express' on May 21 1963, comprising seven Mk I coaches, one of which is still in chocolate/cream livery.** Dave Cobbe Collection/Rail Photoprints

'Centenary' coaches of 1935 but these, most sources agree, were for the 'Cornish Riviera'. Allen also states that the train featured one of the two Diagram H41 'Quick Lunch Buffets', built in 1936 of which No. 9631, at STEAM-Swindon, is the only survivor.

But what, you may ask, about the 'Merchant Venturer'? Or the 'Red Dragon'? Surely, these were classic Western Region named trains?

Yes, they were. But the clue is in the wording 'Western Region'.

BR's regions were given greater flexibility in what colours they could paint locomotives and rolling stock in the mid-1950s. Express passenger engines could receive lined green while coaches for named trains could receive chocolate and cream.

The new livery was adopted for the 'Cornish Riviera Express' (re-named circa 1952) and the 'Torbay Express' in 1956. Trains such as the 'Merchant Venturer', launched as part of the 1951 'Festival of Britain' celebrations, followed. However, the winter 1957/1958 featured a wealth of named trains, many simply given a name in order to justify more coaches being painted in the old GWR colours.

Sadly, for GWR aficionados, most coaches in use on these services were BR Mk Is although GWR-design catering vehicles were still comparatively common. These were gradually replaced as more BR Mk I restaurant/dining cars entered service.

However, that's a bit of a boon for the modeller as Bachmann produces all the Mk I variants required in both its 'OO' gauge Branchline and 'N' gauge Graham Farish ranges. The GWR dining cars will require kit or scratchbuilding for ultimate authenticity.

It's also worth noting that the Western Region re-introduced a Pullman service in 1955, to tap into a commuter traffic between London and South Wales. The 'South Wales Pullman' used a mixture of steel-panelled and match-board cars, all of which Hornby has produced in 'OO' form.

Over these pages, you'll find some sample train formations for the GWR and mid-BR eras. For trains comprising Mk I stock, you'll be able to model them accurately. For GWR-era trains, you'll have to mix and match available (often second-hand) models, bearing in mind that the GWR did not have such a thing as a standard rake of coaches, putting together vehicles of different era, lengths and styles in the same train. That's if you're happy just to use ready-to-run models; a more accurate picture can be formed if you're willing to kit or scratchbuild.

ABOVE: **Here's a scene that could be seen today: Churston is now the engineering headquarters for the Dartmouth Steam Railway while 'Castle' 5043 *Earl of Mount Edgcumbe* is part of the Vintage Trains fleet at Tyseley. But, on June 13 1961, Churston was a wayside station on the Kingswear-Aller Junction branch and 5043 shatters the peace with the 'Torbay Express', bound for Kingswear.** Colour Rail

TEN great modelling projects

Ready-to-run models are great; they're highly detailed and run beautifully. But they do all look the same. So here are ten projects designed to bring a little variety to your fleet.

1. Add those smaller details

Most ready-to-run models come with a small pack of accessories. What you might get depends very much on your chosen model and the scale you model in. A typical 'OO' gauge locomotive might contain bufferbeam pipes, and possibly some etched name and numberplates to replace the printed originals.

But sometimes you need to add a little more to a model to get the best from it. And the beauty of such additions is that can be applied in an evening and needn't cost the earth.

Lamps: All trains required lamps, effectively showing a white light at the front and a red at the rear (be that on the train's last vehicle or the back of the locomotive if running light). But the position of the front lamps was important for they gave an at-a-glance clue as to what the train was. For the subject of this publication, you'll need a lamp on the two outer lamp irons to indicate a Class A (express passenger and, from 1936, empty coaching stock) or a lamp on the top iron, for a Class B (ordinary passenger train). You can buy non-working GWR pattern lamps from ModelU (*www.modelu3d.co.uk*) or Springside (*www.springsidemodels.com*).

Crews: All trains need a driver and fireman and while there are many whitemetal and plastic figures on the market, the most realistic are those from ModelU. Scanned from real people in real poses wearing real uniforms, these are the most realistic figures you can buy. And they're available with all those accruements an engineman needs, such as bags and tea cans. They do need painting though.

Headboards: Premier express trains had names, with a headboard on the locomotive's top lamp iron and roof boards on the coaches. The 'Cheltenham Flyer' headboard was probably the GWR's most elaborate but the Western Region introduced some of the most eye-catching styles. Etched headboards are available from Fox Transfers (*www.fox-transfers.co.uk*)

Lamps, footplate crews and headboards can be fixed into position with a little spot of Deluxe Materials' Tacky Wax (*www.deluxematerials.co.uk/products/tacky-wax*).

ABOVE: **The driver leans from the cab of 'Castle' No. 5079** *Lysander*, **waiting for departure of the 'Torbay Express' in the late 1950s. The locomotive adorned with a headboard and two lamps, on the two outer lamp irons.** Rail Online

2. Reporting numbers

The growth of holiday traffic to the South West placed great demands on the Traffic Department. Trains such as the 'Cornish Riviera' would be run in multiple portions when, at other times of the year, only one train would be required. Therefore, in 1934, the GWR introduced a numbering system to help operating staff identify what the approaching train was. The numbers were carried on a metal frame fixed to the smokebox.

The first number in the original scheme was the originating point of the train: 1XX (Paddington); 2XX (Shrewsbury); 3XX (Wolverhampton/Birmingham); 4XX (Bristol); 5XX (Exeter); 6XX (Plymouth); 7XX (South Wales). Trains starting 0XX were specials while 9XX meant trains originating from the Southern Railway.

The next two numbers were allocated to specific trains. Individual trains would end with either a 0 or a 5. For example, the Down 'Cornish Riviera Limited' was 125, while the 'Torbay Express' was 150. Any relief/separate portion to this main train would then carry the next number in either a '1-4' or '6-9' sequence. For example, a relief to 125 would be 126, while a relief to 150 would be 151. And so on.

These numbers were revised slightly over the years but a big change came in 1959 when the first number became the *destination* point rather than the *originating* point. From 1960, BR's four digit code system was employed although the frames and their numbers continued to be used, the left hand lamp becoming the first 'digit'.

Precision Labels (*www.precisionlabels.com*) offers the frame either as a resin part (which can be permanently fixed with glue or temporarily with Tacky Wax) or a brass part. This just needs folding and painting black. However, installation is a little trickier as you need to glue a small magnet to the inside of the smokebox. However, the individual numbers are magnetic too.

ABOVE: **It's 1950s Paddington and two of the Western Region's premier expresses prepare for departure: a 'King' is in charge of the 'Cornish Riviera Limited' while a 'Castle' is at the head of the 'Cambrian Coast Express'. When the GWR introduced these train reporting boards, locomotive numbers were painted on the bufferbeam. They obscured the BR smokebox numberplates, much to the frustration of many a trainspotter!** Rail Online

3. Improving Hornby's 'Star'

Hornby introduced a concept in 2013 called 'Design Clever', which was created to find ways of reducing the cost of modern model production while maintaining finesse wherever possible. All model trains are hand-built, including all those tiny details, which are cut, fitted and glued by hand. When China became the place to go for mass produced model trains, circa 2000, that meant you could have wonderfully detailed models but, because staff were being paid low wages, the retail price was very competitive.

Demands for increased wages – along with increasing materials costs – meant that those low prices couldn't remain low forever. Rather than put prices up, 'Design Clever' looked at areas where parts could be moulded instead of separately fitted. In some cases, it worked, but in others – smokebox door darts and handrails – it didn't.

The 'Star' of 2013 is a really good model but came on the tail end of 'Design Clever'. Everything about it is to the high standard you'd expect from Hornby, but the cabside handrail is moulded rather than being a separate part. To get the best from the Hornby 'Star', it would be worth cutting away that moulding and replacing it with some fine metal wire. You'll need some fine drill bits in a pin vice to make the mounting holes, some cyanoacrylate, fine wire and fine pliers and some touching up paint.

4. Give 'Truro' a facelift

Another wonderful model that requires a bit of surgery to make it even better is the Bachmann Branchline 'City'. The first fruits of Bachmann working with the National Railway Museum to produce models of locomotives in the National Collection came with the superlative prototype *Deltic* model in 2007. It garnered so many positive reviews that modellers couldn't wait for model number two of the partnership.

It was perhaps no surprise that this was *City of Truro*. The Bachmann/NRM model was unveiled at the Gloucestershire Warwickshire Steam Railway in 2010, complete with a ride behind the real thing.

And what a model it was... or, rather, still is because, 15 years later, it's still in the Bachmann Branchline range. And it's just as good now as it was then. Except for the smokebox door.

Removeable smokebox doors are a common feature nowadays, allowing access to the DCC decoder. The door is often held in place with small magnets.

However, 15-odd years ago, Bachmann started fitting a hinged smokebox door as an additional cosmetic feature, with a moulded tubeplate visible behind. Sadly, adding this feature to 'Truro' meant that its smokebox door doesn't quite match the classic dished shape of the real thing.

Phoenix Precision (*www.phoenix-paints.co.uk*) offers a complete GWR door and door ring. Designed as a replacement for a 'Hall', the diameter should match 'Truro's'. You'll need cutting tools and plenty of filler to remove the original and fit the replacement. Or, if this whitemetal replacement isn't crisp enough for you, you could cut up a donor body from another model... Hornby's take on the GWR smokebox door is one of the best around.

5. Transition era

You'll have probably flicked through this guide and spotted some missing liveries from our livery guides. They are the early British Railways liveries... and they're covered here!

The British Transport Commission had much to organise after British Railways came into being on January 1 1948 . One of those was finding a standard livery for its locomotives.

Initially, Swindon Works painted newly overhauled locomotives in GWR green with a small 'W' – for Western Region – adjacent to the cabside numberplate.

The first trial liveries emerged in mid-1948: 'Kings' 6001/09/25/26 received Ultramarine blue; 'Castles' 4089/91, 5010/21/23/7010/12-13 received Apple green, while Nos. 7008-09, 14-17 received GWR Middle Chrome green and 'Halls' Nos. 5954 and 6910 were painted lined black. All received British Railways lettering with Gill Sans lettering whereas the Middle Chrome Green engines used the GWR's typeface – known as Egyptian - to spell out 'British Railways.'

In 1949, BR decreed that 'Top Link' express engines would receive a blue livery (slightly lighter than Ultramarine) lined with white and black. Secondary passenger engines would be green (often called Brunswick green), lined with orange and black. Mixed traffic and goods engines would receive lined and unlined black, respectively. Express blue would be phased out circa 1952, the 'Kings' gaining BR green; this was applied to the mixed traffic 4-6-0s from 1956 onwards.

So why not bring a little variety to your fleet with an experimental livery or two? Phoenix Precision produces the darker BR blue while you could use its or Railmatch's LNER Doncaster green for the 'Castles'. Fox produces Gill Sans lettering in all three popular scales.

LEFT: This is not the best quality image but it shows the Ultramarine blue applied to four 'Kings' in 1948. The red lining is different to the more well known BR express blue livery. G.W Powell/ Colour Rail

ABOVE: **4091 *Dudley Castle* shows off the experimental apple green livery at Chippenham in 1949.** Kenneth Leech/Colour Rail

ABOVE: The GWR's Egyptian-style typeface was used to spell out 'British Railways' on many locomotives – including 7003 *Elmley Castle* – but the GWR cabside lining was retained. For BR lined green, the lining doesn't go around the cab but cuts across under the windows. Steve Armitage Archive/Rail Online

6. The eight-wheel tender

It's not exactly clear why the GWR built tender No. 2586 in 1931. There's speculation that it was inspired by the eight-wheel tenders that Gresley's LNER 'Pacifics' were running with. It might have offered some advantages of spreading the weight across four axles rather than three.

The body was the same as the Collett 4,000gal but the running gear was different to incorporate the additional axle and the wheel diameter reduced to 3ft 8in. However, the tender weighed 49t 3cwt when fully loaded, three tons heavier than a standard 4,000gal tender.

No. 2586 was initially coupled to 'Hall' 5919 *Worsley Hall* when new in July 1931. It was transferred to 4091 *Dudley Castle* in September 1931 and then 5001 *Llandovery Castle* in October. It also ran at various times with (in numerical order) Nos. 4043/93, 5017/32/49/68/71, 4918, 5957, 6951.

A 4mm:1ft scale kit was offered as part of the Jidenco (later Falcon Brass) range but it's very rare these days. However, an alternative is to contact Stafford Road Models (*www.facebook.com/staffoed.road.models*), which has produced a 3D printed chassis to go with a Hornby or Dapol Collett 4,000gal tender body.

ABOVE: GWR eight-wheel tender 2586 is coupled to 'Castle' 5001 *Llandovery Castle* as it passes Kings Sutton, to the south of Banbury, with an Up express in the early 1930s. P.W. Robinson/Rail Archive Stephenson/Rail Online

7. Build a streamliner

Are you up for a challenge? What about trying to recreate two of the GWR's most eye-catching 4-6-0s?

In this case, eye-catching doesn't mean attractive. Streamlining was at the cutting edge of all forms of transport in the 1930s. Cars started to sport swooping lines while sleek monoplanes were replacing the biplanes of the 1920s. Streamlined diesel trains were appearing in North America and Europe, leaving Britain's railways looking distinctly old fashioned.

The story goes that when GWR senior management learned that the LNER was developing a streamlined steam locomotive, they asked Charles Collett to design a streamliner. Whereas Gresley had experimented with wind tunnels and took best practice from leading streamlining experts, Collett simply stuck Plasticine to a model 'King' and got the Works to copy it.

Consequently, in March, 1935, 'King' 6014 *King Henry IV* and 'Castle' 5005 *Manorbier Castle* appeared, the Plasticine now rendered in steel. They became the Britain's first streamliners, beating the LNER 'A4s' into service by six months. But that's about the only positive thing you could say about them.

Gradually, the streamlined parts were removed until the only traces of the streamlining were No. 5005's cab roof ventilators and No. 6014's wedge-shaped cab.

Creating a GWR streamliner would involve a lot of trial and error, using plastic card and filler (and maybe cutting a small plastic ball in half). But some intrepid modellers have undertaken the challenge to create something truly unusual.

ABOVE: **An ex-works photograph of newly-streamlined 'King' 6014 *King Henry VII*. The continuous splashers would re-appear on the Hawksworth 'Counties.'** Rail Archive Stephenson/Rail Online

8. Improve a County 4-4-0

Despite the myriad 21st century standard models available, visit a model railway show and you'll still see hundreds of older models for sale. They're as cheap as chips and still have plenty of uses... particularly as the subject of detailing projects!

Take the Hornby 'County' 4-4-0, for example. It's a typical 1980s Hornby model. Overall, it looks like the real thing but, closer to, there are a few compromises as it had to fit a standard chassis.

As we explained on p74, it depicts the final batch of curved frame 'Counties.' Surely you can't do anything with it?

Well, David Passingham decided that you could. He turned the Hornby model into a straight-frame version using a razor saw and some plastic card. As David's layout, Maeport East depicts the GWR circa 1905, he's backdated his 'County' to a saturated boiler with no top feed and the safety valves further back.

David cut off the top feed pipe, abrading it flat. The cab was cut and the front curve was also cut away. Replacement frames were made from plastic card. A second cylinder block is needed to donate the piston valves onto the new angled front. David recommends finding line drawings – those in J.H. Russell's *A Pictorial Record of Great Western Engines Vol. 2* are ideal – to judge where to cut the cabsides and the smokebox.

The tender is from a Mainline/Dapol (now Hornby) 'Dean Goods', which is more refined than the one that comes with the Hornby 'County.' David suggests adding new pick-ups to the locomotive and connecting them to the new tender.

You can read more about David's project at *www.gwr.org.uk/pro38xx.html*

ABOVE: **Churchward 'County' 4-4-0 3805 *County Kerry* shows off the straight frames and short smokebox of the early engines outside Swindon Works. It is possible to re-create this series of engines from the Hornby model.** Colour Rail

9. Improve Tri-ang 'Dean Single'

Adding detail to a 1980s model feels achievable… but can you do anything with a model that dates from the 1960s? Yes, says Mikkel Kjartan at *www.gwr.org.uk/pro3031.html* Mikkel uses a Tri-ang 'Dean Single' but these mods could be applied to a more recent Hornby model.

So what mods can you make to such an old model? The Alan Gibson catalogue is your friend here and can provide new handrail knobs and handrails, dome, safety valve bonnet and smokebox door dart. Mikkel also replaced the original bogie wheels with Gibson 14mm bogie wheels. And of course, filling the cut-out in the frame with some plastic card makes a massive visual difference! The tender can be improved by fitting a Dapol 'Dean Goods' tender top and fitting Alan Gibson tender brake rodding and brake shoes.

There are some 1960s aspects of the 'Single' that you can't mask but this is an ideal project if you want to practice your skills.

10. Model the steaming trials

We've talked a lot about the GWR Chief Mechanical Engineers in this publication. But behind every Churchward, Collett or Hawksworth, there were teams of skilled engineers and draughtsmen bringing their visions to reality.

Here, we're talking about the likes of Harold Holcroft or Kenneth Cook. But one engineer that deserves mention is Sam Ell who, after Hawksworth's retirement in 1949, led the campaign to rejuvenate the performance of GWR passenger locomotives. Thanks to the work of Ell and his team, the 'Kings' and 'Castles' began to receive double chimneys while the 'Counties' and the 'Manors' were also transformed.

Swindon Works had had its own testing plant since Churchward's days and under Ell, it came into its own. But trials out on the road were an important part of the testing process too. Locomotives were fitted with monitoring equipment and this was protected – as well as the operatives – by wooden shelters mounted to the front of the locomotive.

You can re-create this key part of the GWR locomotive story in 'OO' gauge thanks to Niu Models, which has produced an indicator shelter kit designed to fit the Hornby 'King'… and you can do for less than a tenner and with minimal tools. Order from *www.niumodels.co.uk*

ABOVE: **'County' 1009 *County of Carmarthen* carries an indicator shelter to monitor its steaming, having now been fitted with a trial chimney, at Swindon Works in November 1954.** Rail Online

Recommended reading

Want to know more about GWR express and passenger locomotives? Here's what you need on your bookshelf.

The challenge with putting together a guide such as this is what do you include and what do you leave out? Locomotive history include lots of technical information, which is of more use to the historian and engineer than the modeller. We've done our best to include everything that is relevant to the modeller, although covering the best part of 20 classes means that there are likely to be some omissions.

Guides such as this one act as a starting point. If you want to know more about a particular class, it's always recommended to buy a book on the subject.

Here's what we've used putting this guide together (as well as Vols 1 & 2 of the 9th edition of *Ramsay's British Model Trains*), although it goes without saying that there are many more out there, either new or second-hand. But if you want a good starting point to enter the world of GWR locomotive development and GWR operation, here's our shortlist.

A Pictorial Record of Great Western Engines Vol 2 by J.H. Russell (Oxford Publishing Company)

A Pictorial Record of Great Western Coaches Part 2 by J.H. Russell (Oxford Publishing Company)

An Outline of GW Locomotive Practice by Harold Holcroft (Locomotive Publishing Company)

Atlantic Era by Martin Evans (Percival Marshall)

BR Steam In Colour 1948-1968 by Colin Boocock (Ian Allan)

C.B. Collett – A Competent Successor by J.E. Chacksfield (Oakwood Press)

Churchward Locomotives by Brian Haresnape and Alec Swain (Ian Allan)

Collett & Hawksworth Locomotives by Brian Haresnape (Ian Allan)

Freddy And The Jets by Chris Leigh (*Model Rail*, April 2007)

GWR Two Cylinder 4-6-0s & 2-6-0s by Rodger Bradley (David & Charles)

GWR Locomotive Allocations by J.W.P. Rowledge (David & Charles)

Great Western 4-6-0s At Work by Michael Rutherford (Promotional Reprint Company)

Great Western 'Saint' Class 4-6-0 by O.S. Nock (Patrick Stephens)

Nostalgic Days & Footplate Days by Harold Gasson (Oxford Publishing Company)

Portraits of Western 4-6-0s by Bryan Holden & Kenneth H. Leech (Fraser Stewart)

Speed Records on Britain's Railways by O.S. Nock (Pan Books)

Standard Gauge Great Western 4-4-0s by O.S. Nock (David & Charles)

The Book of the Castle 4-6-0s by Ian Sixsmith (Irwell Press)

The Book of the King 4-6-0s by Ian Sixsmith (Irwell Press)

The Book of the County 4-6-0s by Ian Sixsmith (Irwell Press)

The Book of the Hall 4-6-0s Part 4 by Ian Sixsmith (Irwell Press)

The GWR Stars, Castles & Kings (Omnibus Edition) by O.S. Nock (David & Charles)

The Great Western Railway in the 1930s Vols 1 & 2 by David Geen & Barry Scott (Kingfisher Railway Productions)

The Great Western Coaches 1890-1954 by Michael Harris (David & Charles)

The Locomotives of the Great Western Railway Part 8 (RCTS)

Titled Trains of Great Britain by C.J. Allen (Ian Allan)

ABOVE: **'Castle' 4094 *Dynevor Castle* nears Denham/West Ruislip with an Up express for Paddington on August 14 1954.** C.R.L. Coles/Dave Cobbe Collection/Rail Photoprints